AN INTRODUCTION TO
THE EXPERIMENTAL
PSYCHOLOGY OF BEAUTY

BY

C. W. VALENTINE, M.A., D.Phil.

PROFESSOR OF EDUCATION IN THE QUEEN'S UNIVERSITY OF BELFAST,
FORMERLY LECTURER IN EXPERIMENTAL PSYCHOLOGY TO THE
ST. ANDREWS PROVINCIAL COMMITTEE FOR THE
TRAINING OF TEACHERS

REVISED EDITION

London and Edinburgh:
T. C. & E. C. JACK, LTD. | T. NELSON & SONS, LTD.
1919

2441

PREFACE TO FIRST EDITION.

In this little book I have attempted to give an account of some experiments dealing with the psychology of the appreciation of beauty. An effort has been made to render every page intelligible to the general reader, and no previous knowledge of psychology is necessary. A few paragraphs less simple than the rest have been enclosed in square brackets. These can be omitted if desired, without the general drift of ideas being lost.

It is only within recent years that men have attempted to apply the method of experiment to the processes of the mind, and of such work experiments dealing with our appreciation of beauty form only one section. Yet such is the enthusiasm with which the subject has been taken up by a number of investigators, that it will be impossible for the writer, in such a small book as this, to give a full account of all the results obtained.

An attempt to give a bald summary of the results of all the experiments would probably have confused the novice, for whom this book is intended. I have thought it better, therefore, to deal in each chapter fairly fully with two or three typical and important series of experiments, grouping a number of supplementary experimental results about these. I have ventured to include among these a number of my own experiments, most of them hitherto unpublished. I regret that lack of space has prevented me from referring, except very briefly here and there, to musical experiments.

My best thanks are due to Professor Stout, who first suggested that I should deal with the psychology of æsthetics, and who has occasionally discussed with me some of the problems here mentioned ; to Mr. E. Bullough of Gonville and Caius College, Cambridge, for a critical reading of the typoscript, and also for the great help which I have derived from his published articles ; and to my wife, for frequent assistance in dealing with materials obtained from my own experiments.

C. W. V.

PREFACE TO SECOND EDITION.

In this new edition two chapters have been added on Music and Rhythm, and a number of emendations and additions have been made elsewhere. I am indebted to Dr. C. S. Myers, Editor of the *British Journal of Psychology*, for permission to quote freely from some articles of mine in that journal, and to Mr. G. Fitzsimons, Mus. Bac., for a critical reading of the chapters on Music and Rhythm.

C. W. V.

QUEEN'S UNIVERSITY
OF BELFAST.

CONTENTS.

THE EXPERIMENTAL PSYCHOLOGY OF BEAUTY.

CHAPTER I.

INTRODUCTORY.

A VERY distinguished psychologist indeed has asserted his belief that psychology may enunciate truths which may help the artist in his creative work. But so complex is the mind of man that, in the present stage of the development of the science, the psychologist can hardly hope to instruct an artist of real power how better to do his work, though the artist may be led to understand more fully the reasons *why* certain things which he has done "instinctively," as we say, were good things to do, and why things he avoided would have spoilt the beauty of his work and the pleasure of those who saw it.

Some practical value from the study of the psychology of beauty may be derived by those who instruct the young in art or seek to develop their appreciation of beauty. An understanding, for example, of why certain kinds of things appeal most to children, and of the line of development from the attitude of the child, towards the various forms of beauty, to the attitude adopted by the adult, should be of value to the educator.

The main value of experimental æsthetics, however, is the interest which lies in the subject itself. To understand something more of the mysteries of the mind of man should be of interest for us, even if we cannot go deeply into them. Nor is it merely the unusual that is wonderful. The ordinary everyday working of the mind is not without its wonders, though so many people only think it extraordinary if something goes wrong. Such people readily marvel at the fact that a man has lost his memory of the past, even of his own name. Deeper reflection will show that the miracle is that we *do* remember our names or anything at all. Thus in our psychological investigations we shall not confine ourselves to the exceptional, which, though it naturally strikes our attention more forcibly than what is usual, is really no more wonderful and no harder to explain.

Beauty and Pleasure.—The reader will find that there is frequent reference to the question whether colours, pictures, &c., are pleasing or displeasing. It must not, however, be imagined that the appreciation of beauty and the enjoyment of pleasure are regarded as one and the same thing. Pathos may add beauty to a picture or to a symphony, and it is obvious that there is a great deal more than pleasure in the full appreciation of a tragedy, whether it be represented in drama or on canvas.

This is not the place to discuss what exactly is implied in the term beauty. That is for the æsthetician proper. But it is widely admitted that, in general, the enjoyment of beauty is accompanied by pleasure, and in particular the pleasure aspect is especially predominant when we are concerned with such elements as colour, line, &c. The experiments described in the first part of this book deal chiefly with these elements. It has been found more convenient in such psychological experiments to ask persons the question, " Do you like this, and if so, why ? " or " Do you find this pleasing ? " rather than "Do you think this beautiful, and why ? " The last question too often tends to result in a discussion as to the application of the term beautiful.

In applying the **Method of Experiment** to the study of our appreciation of the beautiful, it is well to commence with simple elements. For example, we may first take a number of single colours, or of uncoloured lines or figures, and see how people are affected by them. A picture involves so many complex features, such as colour, form, meaning, association, memory of the original (if a copy), knowledge of the artist's reputation, or of his other work, and so on. Now all these points are of great interest, but it is difficult to say to what extent each factor is of influence in determining our judgment of the whole. By taking simple colours or forms, however, we reduce the number of these complexities, though we do not by any means get rid of them all. More especially we are able to vary simple objects, such as coloured papers or lines, in many different ways, and to see how these variations affect the observer. Thus we may hope, in time, to learn all that can be learned about the beauty of that kind of object as it appeals to men in its isolated form. Afterwards we may have a better chance of dealing with more complex objects into which the colours or forms enter as constituent elements. Of course we shall find great changes in the effects of colours or lines when they are built up into complex arrangements such as pictures. But we may reasonably expect some of their most striking and characteristic effects to remain even then. And we also sometimes find similar mental attitudes when a person looks at a picture, or listens to a sonata, as occur when he looks at a single colour or hears a single chord. Thus in studying the enjoyment of simple objects and their effects we are really studying, given the right attitude on the part of the observer, a very much simplified æsthetic experience.

CHAPTER II.

THE BEAUTY OF COLOUR.

THE great power of colour as an element of beauty is a matter of common knowledge. Some have thought that the influence of colour can be traced to associations built up in our own experience. Thus the red and yellow are said to impress us as warm colours, because they have been associated often with the light of the sun or the heat of the fire; green may be said to appear restful to the busy townsman, because associated with the quiet peace of the country, and so on. Many facts and experiments, however, seem to show that the influence of colours cannot be entirely traced to associations, but that they have a direct stimulating or depressing effect upon us, which is something more deep-seated than the most frequent associations.

As we shall see, different colours have different effects on infants only a few months old, to an extent which we can scarcely ascribe to any associations within their short range of experience—indeed before we have any evidence that associations with colours have taken place. Again, in the recent case of a man who had been blind from birth until a cataract was removed, it was found that red was at once pleasing to him, whilst yellow made him feel exceedingly sick. In this case, of course, no associations could explain these different effects. Different coloured lights, indeed, affect even animals in different ways. The exciting properties of red upon some animals are well known. Even low types of animal life, where there is apparently no vision, are sensitive to different colours and react upon them in different ways. Thus the amœba turns away from blue, as it does from white light, but does not turn from red. One experimenter placed an equal number of earthworms in two boxes, one light, the other dark, with an opening between, and the number in each box was counted every hour. It was found after a time that there were five times as many worms in the light box as in the dark. In an exactly similar way it was shown that they preferred red to green, and green to blue. Yet earthworms probably receive their light impressions through the skin, it being doubtful whether they have any visual organs proper. If such low types of animal life feel differently towards different colours, we shall not be surprised to find that the highly sensitive human organism is also directly affected by colours, apart from their associations.

The general stimulating effect of colour, and of some colours in particular, was wonderfully demonstrated in some experiments by a French doctor, Féré. He used an instrument which recorded the strength of the handgrip. He ascertained first the normal handgrip of various individuals, and then their grip under the influence of various coloured lights. The differences produced by the various colours were especially striking in the case of a hysteric subject. If his normal handgrip is represented by the number 23, then it was found that blue caused a grip represented by 24, green by 28, yellow 30, orange 35, and red 42. It was found, too, that the circulation of the blood was affected, as was shown by the variations in the volume of the forearm. Thus we see that colours affect us in a way that extends even to the stimulation of the muscular and circulatory systems, and that the colours at the "warm" end of the spectrum are the most stimulating.

Colour Preferences among Children.—When we

come to test the colour preferences of very young
children, we find that it is these more stimulating
colours that are preferred. Several careful experimenters have concluded that infants of a year old,
or even as young as seven months, already show a
marked preference for red and yellow before other
colours, and even before white, though infants are
notoriously attracted by brightness. Some of these
experiments were carried out as follows. Two coloured
blocks of wood or pieces of paper would be placed at
an equal distance from the child, and a record made
as to which object he grasped at. The tendency to
use the right (or left) hand more than the other was
allowed for by presenting, say, the red first on the
child's right, with the blue on the left, and afterwards reversing the position of the coloured blocks.
The present writer carried out a series of experiments
by a new method, extending over five weeks, upon his
little boy, at a considerably younger age, when he
was only three and a half months old. A detailed
description of the method, which requires many precautions, has been published elsewhere, but the experiments may be shortly described here. The infant
was placed comfortably among cushions, and two
coloured wools were held by the writer about a foot
and a half in front of him, and about one foot apart,
against the dull grey background of the experimenter's coat. It was easy for me to see when the
child gazed at either colour, and I called out the
name of the colour looked at, or " off " when the
child removed his gaze from it. The exact moments
of these actions were recorded by an assistant with
the aid of a watch indicating seconds, so that the
length of time each colour was looked at could be
calculated afterwards. When the two colours had
been so held for two minutes, after an interval the
position of the colours was reversed, and another

two minutes was given. On another day two other colours were given, and so on until each of the nine colours had been presented with each of the others, involving seventy-two experiments of two minutes each. Care was taken to spread the colours fairly evenly over the whole series to avoid monotony. The total amount of time during which the child looked at any given colour was added, ignoring times less than three seconds. [By comparing the scores of each colour with the totals scored by the other colours when they were paired with it we allow for variations of mood and interest on the part of the child. Hence the scores of each colour are given as percentages of the total amount of time that either colour was looked at while the given colour was being presented.] The following were the results approximately : yellow, 80 per cent. ; white, 74 per cent. ; pink, 72 per cent. ; red, 45 per cent. ; brown, 37 per cent. ; black, 35 per cent. ; blue, 29 per cent. ; green, 28 per cent. ; violet, 9 per cent. I may add that the child was obviously fascinated by yellow, white, and pink, sometimes gazing at one colour for as long as a minute at a time. He was also obviously bored with green, blue, and violet. Of course the yellow and pink were much brighter than the other colours—*i.e.* there was more white in them. The high position of these colours and of white confirms the results of other observers, that infants are greatly attracted by brightness. If we refer the position of white, yellow, and pink partly to their brightness, we get a result which is not unlike that of Féré. One cannot, of course, generalise upon one set of experiments, especially when they are so difficult to carry out as is the case with very young infants. But the results given by experiments upon other children agree with mine in suggesting that in the early months of life the most attractive colours are those at the " warm " end of the spectrum, which Féré found to be the most stimulating colours.

This preference seems to continue for a time into early boyhood and girlhood, and then the other colours tend to become more popular. In Antwerp, experiments upon many school children showed that red was the most popular colour with children from four to nine years of age, whilst after that age blue was the most popular. Mr. W. H. Winch made experiments upon 2000 school children in London, ages seven to fifteen, asking them to write down the following colours—white, black, red, green, yellow, and blue—in the order in which they liked them. With the youngest children (Standard I.) red was the most popular colour, as it was in Standards II., III., and IV., in one of the boys' schools. Yellow generally dropped from second or third place with the youngest children to fourth or even fifth place with the oldest. Blue, after the 1st Standard, usually takes the first place, and green moves from its usual position of fourth or even fifth with the youngest children to third or even second with the oldest. Mr. Winch gives as the average girl's order of preference : blue, red, white, green, yellow, black ; for the boys' : blue, red, green, yellow, white, black.

Already, then, with school children we have passed the stage at which stimulation is the supreme factor in determining the attractiveness of a colour. Green was much more popular in a school with rural surroundings than in the city schools, and this is attributed in part to the influence of the foliage and green grass. White is more popular with the girls, especially the older ones, than with the boys, possibly on account of the frequent use and suitability of white for dress. Thus, even at this early age, experience and associations begin to modify the original effect

(2,008)

of colours, and this process doubtless goes on far into adult life.

Colour Preferences among Adults.—An experimenter who found that white, red, and yellow were especially preferred by American students, in explaining this, refers to a modern theory of colour vision. [She writes, " According to the Hering theory of colour, white, red, and yellow are the so-called ' dissimilating ' colours in the three pairs, white-black, red-green, and yellow-blue, corresponding to the three hypothetical visual substances in the retina. These substances, that is, in undergoing a kind of chemical disintegration under the action of light-rays, are supposed to give the sensations white, red, or yellow respectively, and in renewing themselves again to give the sensations of black, green, and blue. The dissimilating process seems to bring about stronger reactions on the physiological side, as if it were a more exciting process. Thus it is found that as measured by the increase in strength of the handgrip under the stimulation of various colours, red has particularly exciting qualities, but the other colours have an analogous effect, lessening, however, with the descent from red to violet. The pleasure in bright red, or yellow, for instance, may thus well be the feeling-tone arising in the purely physiological effect of the colour. If red works like a trumpet call, while blue calms and cools, and if red is preferred to blue, it is because a sharp stimulation is so felt, and so preferred."]

It does not, however, seem that the preference for such stimulating colours is by any means uniform among adults. In some further experiments with adults Mr. Winch found that green came second on the average with women and first with men, and the popularity of green with adults often seems to be due in part actually to its restfulness. In general it is characteristic of the little child, as of the savage, to like striking, stimulating sensations ; witness their fondness for loud sounds as well as for " loud " colours. With age, experience, and culture, the finer shades and variations come to be more fully appreciated, and the immediate " physiological " effect (if we may use the term somewhat slackly) is overlaid with a multitude of complications which may almost obscure it entirely. An unpleasant association, for example, may spoil an otherwise pleasing colour for us perhaps for life.

In view of the enormous variations of such influences of experience upon different individuals, it is scarcely possible to make a satisfactory statement as to the most popular colours with adults. Mr. Winch, using the same methods as in his experiments with children, found that the average order for twenty-four men (average age twenty-eight years) and for forty-one women (average age thirty years) was as follows :

Men.	*Women.*
Green.	Blue.
Blue.	Green.
Red.	White.
White.	Red.
Yellow.	Yellow.
Black.	Black.

These lists obviously do not agree with the statement that the " stimulating " colours, red and yellow, are most popular. Indeed, in view of the enormous differences between the environment and experiences of different individuals (apart from the question of congenital differences) it is, perhaps, scarcely possible to make a sweeping statement as to what colours are most popular with adults. We can say much more, as we shall see, as to what *char-*

acteristics of any or all of the colours are pleasing or displeasing.

Furthermore, it is difficult to compare the results of different experiments upon colour, owing to the great effect of slight variations of shade and saturation of the colours used by different experimenters. Mr. Winch's subjects (*i.e.* the persons on whom the experiments were performed) were at liberty to think of any shade they chose, while the American subjects had coloured papers of specific shades presented to them. The blues and greens in the American experiments might have been somewhat unpleasant shades of blue or green, while the reds and yellows might have been particularly pleasing shades. (This difficulty can now be removed by the use of standard colours and wools which are issued especially for experimental purposes.)

Further, we do not yet know how far nationality, with its varying environment, may affect colour preferences. We know that the southern nations of Europe and tropical peoples seem to prefer warmer and more striking colours than do the people of the colder north. Nor does this appear to be merely a question of degree of culture. The educated women of Germany are fonder of strong, intense colours than the women of Scotland appear to be.

Such facts as these must be taken into consideration in comparing the results of experiments in different countries. We must not assume that different series of experiments are valueless because they happen to give different results.

That custom and habit may markedly affect the popularity of a colour is shown by the changes of fashion. A colour really comes to appear more pleasing to many when it has been approved for a time as fashionable. Thus we may even expect some variations in the colour preferences of people of the same country at different periods.

Sub-conscious Associations.—We have tried to show that colours have an effect on us due to their own nature, and not merely to the association of objects or experiences connected with them. At the same time we find that such associations play an important part, especially with some people, in determining the attitude adopted towards a given colour. In the first place there are probably deep-set associations whose origins we have long forgotten. The pleasure of a given blue may be due to the faint revival of many happy experiences under blue skies, though we may not remember them, and may not even think of a blue sky. Experiments have shown that we may have a feeling, similar to one we experienced when we saw a given object, even when that object itself is not recalled. Thus we cannot necessarily conclude that vague associations are not at work when a colour pleases us, merely because we cannot trace them. Perhaps we may speak of these as sub-conscious associations.

General Associations.—Under this heading we may include those associations of which we are conscious, but which are not dependent upon experiences which are particularly and peculiarly our own. For example, several of my subjects expressed a liking for colours because they are found in nature. A definite shade of blue may remind anyone of the sky, and a red quite commonly suggests a railway signal.

Individual Associations. — On the other hand, the pleasingness or otherwise of a colour is sometimes due to a quite special and individual experience of the observer. Thus one of my subjects disliked a colour because it was the colour of a flower disliked when she was a child ; another liked a colour because it was his " political " colour, a general election being in progress at the time of the experiments. An even more remote association was that in the case of a subject who disliked a colour because it was the colour of a tie constantly worn by a teacher whom she had greatly disliked! In such cases the subject may be quite unable to get rid of the associations, though he may recognise that he is not justified in calling a colour ugly or beautiful for such reasons. The distinction between general and individual associations in this sense is convenient though not absolute. Many associations lie upon the border, and there is a gradual transition from one class to another.

When one of my subjects was asked which she preferred of two colours, A, a royal blue, and B, a faded yellow-green, she declared that she preferred B. The faded green reminded her of autumn, and this made her dislike A, " because it is never seen in autumn." Here we have a case where an association, with a given colour B, determines a person's attitude not only to the colour itself, but to another colour seen at the same time. In this case the association was strong enough to put a dirty yellow-green, disliked by almost everyone to whom I showed it, before a highly popular blue.

A different association might have reversed the judgment. Thus one subject to whom I presented two colours, E and F, expressed a preference for E, because it suggested a lily. Then she wrote, " When I found I was not really comparing the two colours before me I tried to compare them again. But this time I thought of two blouses made of the two given colours, and now I preferred F, because E would not suit me." Thus we see how very inconstant are the influences of associations.

An interesting example of associations bound up with colour is found where we connect other sensations with colour, as when we speak of a colour being heavy, or light, or too sweet. It is well known that, in general, a dark colour looks better below a light one than above it. If the wall of a staircase is to be papered with two different coloured papers we prefer the lower half of the wall to have the darker shade. Otherwise it would look top-heavy. This apparent **heaviness of colours** has been investigated by Mr. E. Bullough, who has done the most important experimental work in the æsthetics of colour in this country. He used triangles, circles, or squares of coloured paper, the top " half " being of one colour, the lower of a different colour, or at least of a different shade.

Two triangles, such as are shown in Fig. 1, were presented, and the subject was asked which he preferred and why. Fifty subjects were tested. It was found that in most cases the " weight-principle " determined the preference, *i.e.* subjects liked the triangle in which the darker shade or colour was at the base of the

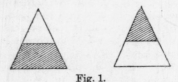

Fig. 1.

triangle. The influence of the " weight-principle " was much more constant when the two parts of the triangle were coloured with different shades of the same colour rather than with different tones. In many cases, but not all, subjects were able to trace their preferences to this " weight-principle," even if they had never thought of it before. When asked why some colours should appear heavier than others, most subjects were at a loss for a reason. Some suggested that it was due to association, that " being constantly surrounded by natural objects which were of a darker colour below than above (*e.g.* trees and mountains), we had contracted the habit of considering this arrangement as typical, and expected to find it conformed to in other objects which, as the triangles for instance, do not form part of our customary environment."

But Mr. Bullough showed that there were two objections to this theory. In the first place, the arrangement of natural objects is by no means so uniformly like that suggested. "We may find a cornfield in the foreground with a dark wood behind it quite as often as a meadow with a corn or clover field beyond." There are white cottages with thatched or tiled roofs. Even if the arrangement of light over dark is usual in nature, it does not seem sufficiently uniform to account for the fact that very slight differences of shade influenced the preferences given.

There was a second reason against this explanation. A number of the subjects were specially liable to form associations between the coloured figures and landscapes or seascapes : thus the circle with the lower half green and the upper half blue suggested the sea with the sky above. Now it was found that there was a curious antagonism between these landscape associations and the weight-principle. Scarcely ever was there an associated suggestion of a landscape when the weight-principle was at work. And on the few occasions when the two were found together they were actually opposed in their influence, *i.e.* the weight-principle would make triangle A preferred, but the suggestion of landscape made B preferable.

Associations of this kind, then, seem inadequate to explain the fact that we like to have dark colours below light ones, rather than vice versa. Mr. Bullough points out that in the case of red and pink, the addition of more red to the pink makes it more and more like the red : in other words, in the red there appears to be more pigment than in the pink. And in adding red to pink we make it darker. "Dark red, therefore, compared with saturated red, has again this peculiar quality of moreness" ; it has more substance, *i.e.* it appears heavier.

Some other interesting points came to light in these experiments with the coloured triangles. The weight-principle was not always supreme. Selections were sometimes made on the basis of a preference for one of the two colours in the triangle. Thus suppose the triangle A to be composed of light green in the lower part and dark blue in the apex, while the triangle B had green at the apex and blue below. Then the triangle A might be preferred to B, because A had *more* of the colour green in it than B had, the subject having a strong liking for green but not for dark blue. Here the weight-principle would have led to the choice of B, where the dark blue was below the light green.

With other subjects, again, the triangle which had the favourite colour in the apex was preferred, even if this were the darker colour, for they felt that the apex was the dominant, important position, and thus their favourite colour appeared more prominent and striking in this position.

This influence of position and arrangement upon the effect of a colour will obviously affect the beauty of more complex objects, such as paintings. The greater importance of a small object in a picture may make up for the greater area of the less important background. Thus a picture in which a small central figure is of a highly pleasing colour, but the broad background in colour of an indifferent nature, may be more pleasing than another painting in which the body of a picture is of a pleasing colour but where the principal figure is poorly coloured. The greatest perfection is required where one's attention naturally lingers most readily, just as in photography we must focus the camera most carefully for the object of main interest; this, above all else, must come out clear and distinct in the picture even if larger objects of secondary importance are blurred.

So great does this effect of the position of a colour seem to have been with some subjects that it actually caused an illusion. Thus the red appeared to one subject more glaring in the square in which it was uppermost than in the square in which it was below. Yet, as a matter of fact, the colours were exactly the same. Such illusions occurred with ten out of the fifty persons taking part in the experiments.

The Influence of the Area of a Coloured Surface.—The extent to which the area of a coloured surface affects the pleasingness of a colour has also been investigated recently. Thirty-three American women were tested with coloured squares of 5 and 25 cms. square respectively. The colours used were saturated red, orange, yellow, green, blue and violet, and also light tints and dark shades of each of these. It was found that the small squares of the saturated colours were generally preferred to the large squares, except in the case of red, where the large square was preferred. In the case of the light tints of the various colours, there was a slight tendency for the larger squares to be preferred. In the case of the dark shades there was a very decided preference for the large squares before the small ones, the tendency to prefer the larger area being less marked in the case of green and violet. Of course, in such experiments a great deal will obviously depend upon the actual colours which are best liked by the subjects tested. If we have a strong dislike to a colour, as a rule we shall be more pleased the less we see of it, whereas we are glad to see plenty of a pleasing colour. This, however, is not the only principle at work, for, as the experiments show, there are cases where a colour is very pleasing in a small area but not so pleasing in a large area, and these in general are naturally the more intense colours. Thus we saw that the saturated colours are preferred in the small areas, rather than in the large, with the exception of the red. And it is noticeable that red was, with these subjects, the most popular of all the saturated colours used. So here the desire to have plenty of a pleasing colour would enter in.

Again, it is comprehensible that the larger areas of the tints and shades (as distinguished from the saturated colours) should be preferred, at least in the case of those colours which are liked. For the indefiniteness of the colour of an object, any uncertainty as to its actual colour-tone is lessened by an increase in the size of the coloured area, and the stimulating effect is probably in most cases increased.

It has also been found that the length of time a colour is looked at affects its pleasingness for us. Experiments were performed by Miss Washburn upon fourteen women, with eighteen different colours. A colour was exposed for one minute, and the subject had to say whether her feeling towards the colour changed at all during that time. It was found that in the vast majority of cases some change did occur. The changes were of two main kinds :

1. There were changes in the apparent colour, the colour apparently fading or getting darker. This is due to what is known as " adaptation " of the eye. There were also " after-images," which any reader may observe by gazing steadily at a colour and then looking away at some neutral tint, or at the white ceiling. The presence of an after-image almost invariably lessened the pleasure derived from the colour. With the saturated colours " adaptation was favourable to violet, blue, and green, but un-

favourable to red and yellow. It had no effect upon the pleasingness of orange." In other words, colours at the warm (red) end of the spectrum were liked at least as well in their original saturation as in the duller tones produced by adaptation. Naturally adaptation was more unfavourable to the dark shades and dark tints, these colours being already too faint to allow of any further weakening without a loss of pleasingness.

2. Secondly, there were changes in the mental attitude towards the colours. Sometimes subjects found that they became tired of the colour, especially of the dark shades and saturated colours—very rarely of the light tints. On the other hand, a colour occasionally became more pleasing as it was looked at longer, the subject saying that " she was getting used to it." Again, associations often cropped up within the minute, and influenced the judgment upon the colour.

Associations had not much effect upon the saturated colours—which is not surprising, as they do not occur very frequently in nature, or indeed in dress or any of the things of everyday life. With the dark shades and light tints, associations had generally a favourable influence. Of course the prolonged looking at a colour for one minute would give ample opportunity for associations to occur. But other experiments in which colours were exposed for only a fraction of a second have shown that associations may occur even within such a short time.

CHAPTER III.

THE BEAUTY OF COLOUR (*continued*).

WE have several times had to call attention to individual differences among people as regards their attitude towards colours. It may be well now to discuss these differences more fully. Mr. E. Bullough in an important series of experiments has shown that many individuals can be classified into types according to their usual way of regarding colours. In these experiments seventy different shades of colours were used, and thirty-five subjects (three of whom were women) were tested. The experiments took place in a dark room, artificial light being used in order to avoid the variations of daylight. The subject looked through a circular hole at the illuminated coloured paper, and was asked to state whether he liked or disliked the colour, and particularly to give his reason for liking or disliking it. Now it is quite true that we are often quite unable to say why we like or dislike a colour, and it is probably true that no one is able to give all the reasons that help to determine the exact effect that a colour has upon him, for, as we saw, many sources of our feeling may be buried in experiences long since forgotten. But it seems fair to suppose, that in so far as reasons can be discovered by self-examination, those which are most influential in determining our preference will in the long run attract attention most readily and most frequently.

It was found that the reasons given showed that **different aspects of colour** appeal strongly to different people. These aspects of colour, or ways of regarding them, are four in number, illustrated by the following judgments actually given by some of the subjects :—

(I.) *Objective Aspect.*—Colours found pleasing because saturated, pure, bright ; or displeasing because too thin, mixed, dull, foggy, and so on. Here the attention is fixed upon the colour itself, and on its qualities as a colour.

(II.) *Physiological Aspect.*—A colour is found pleasing because stimulating, soothing, warming; or displeasing because dazzling, depressing, or because it "makes one feel hot." Here the attention is drawn towards the effect of the colour upon the subject himself, particularly to its effect upon his bodily organism. How marked such effects may be we saw illustrated by Féré's experiments upon the effect of colours upon the strength of the handgrip.

(III.) *Associative Aspect.*—With this we are already familiar. The pleasingness of a colour is determined by the things of which it reminds the subject.

(IV.) *Character Aspect.*—Colours liked because jovial, fearless, energetic, truthful, sympathetic ; or disliked because stubborn, treacherous, too aggressive, and so forth. In these judgments we find the colour regarded and spoken of almost as if it were a person. A *character* is attributed to it.

Now it was found that most of the subjects were especially attracted by some one of these aspects of colour. As a rule, of course, a subject gave examples of several of these kinds of judgments, but generally he approximated to a type, according to whether most of his judgments referred to the objective, physiological, associative, or character aspect of the colours. The types may be described in fuller detail.

Objective Type.—People of this type took up an intellectual and critical attitude towards the colours rather than an emotional attitude. The tendency to analyse the colour, to find in it traces of another colour, and so to judge it impure, is typical of this class. People of this critical type were more apt to dislike the colours than were those of the other types. They gave the experimenter the impression that they could not get into an intimate relation with colours. They rarely seem to have any marked and consistent preferences for certain colours before others, though they often have some fixed standard according to which they judge colours.

The Physiological Type.—People of this type are especially sensitive to the stimulating and warming, or soothing and cooling properties of a colour. Frequently, then, they have a consistent preference for reds and greens, according to whether they prefer to be stimulated or soothed. One subject of this type actually shivered when he saw a particularly cold blue. This type on the whole is more appreciative of colours than are people of the objective type. Yet the æsthetic enjoyment of the colours is lessened in so far as attention is called away from the colour to the effect it is producing on the observer himself.

The Associative Type.—This formed a somewhat smaller class than the physiological type, and the subjects of this type almost invariably gave some " objective " and " physiological " judgments as well. As to their abstract colour-preferences persons of this type will obviously vary very much, according to the kind of associations to which they are particularly liable. Thus those who are constantly reminded of nature will like best perhaps green ; a woman who is frequently reminded of dress will like those colours which she is fond of wearing because they suit her, and so forth.

All the three women were of the associative type. The number is, of course, far too small upon which to base any conclusion. But I may add that in some of my own colour experiments I found that six men only gave one associative reason, while twenty women contributed ten cases of associations.

Mr. Bullough raises the important question as to the æsthetic value of associations, and contends that this depends upon " the degree of fusion which can be reached by the individual between the colour impression and the associated content." But for a discussion of this we must refer the reader to Mr. Bullough's own writings.

The Character Type.—Only three of the thirty-five subjects were pure examples of this type, though a number seemed to be transition cases from the physiological to the character type. People of this type differ from those of the objective type by being far more appreciative of colours. The critical attitude gives place to a lively sympathy. As we saw, they read feeling or character of almost a human nature into the colours, finding them cheerful or sad, bold or gentle, honest or untrustworthy. Obviously their description of colours will sometimes resemble those of the physiological type. The difficulty, for example, occurred as to whether the comment " cheerful " meant that the colour itself was cheerful (character type) or that it made the observer feel cheerful (physiological type). In these cases the subject was asked for an explanation, and generally they were very decided, some emphatically asserting that it was the colour itself that appeared cheerful, not that it made *them* feel cheerful, while to others it appeared absurd to speak of a colour being itself cheerful.

It was remarkable that the characters attributed to the same colour by different and quite independent observers were often exceedingly similar. The following are examples of comments upon several colours, each made by a different subject. Orange : " mysterious," " undecided," " delicate," " mystic."

Saturated red : "strong and dashing," "violent," "boisterous," "self-sufficient, grand, and majestic," "cheerful and lively," "active and sympathetic." Unsaturated blue : "simplicity, soothing," "restful, lacking energy," "nondescript," "undecided," "morbid." In general red tones appeared sympathetic, open, frank and even "gushing," blues being more reserved and distant, though not necessarily disliked on that account. Yellow is essentially cheerful and "light of heart," with a tendency to frivolity. Green as opposed to yellow was solid and even "bourgeois"; as contrasted with red, restful; as distinguished from blue, jovial instead of reserved. But the slightest tinge of yellow or blue in green greatly affected its character.

The combination in purple of the two colours red and blue, so different in their character aspect, leads to interesting comments : blue purple was the mystic, unfathomable colour, and was described by one subject as a "person with a past"; while red purple combines something of the strength of red with the "thoughtfulness" of blue.

The interesting question arises as to which type of person or judgment represents the highest stage of æsthetic development. I will only state that Mr. Bullough gives the following order, based largely upon the degree to which the subject thinks of the beauty of the colour, as a quality of the colour itself, not of something connected with it, or merely as a cause of a pleasurable feeling in the observer. Lowest in the scale comes the pure "physiological" type, in which the subject thinks chiefly of the pleasure or displeasure he experiences. Second come the nonfused associative judgments, in which the associations are more remote, including those we have called individual associations. Third comes the objective type, where, it is true, the attention is fixed upon the colour itself and its qualities as such, but in which the attitude is too critical and aloof to reach the highest degree of æsthetic value. Fourth come the " fused " associations, and highest of all the character type.

It was found that these different types of judgments persisted when subjects had to express their opinions upon **combinations of two colours,** and here the character type was more numerous, including twelve subjects out of forty, and the associative type much less numerous (four out of forty).

There is not space to give the many kinds of reasons given to explain the pleasingness or otherwise of various combinations. I should like, however, to mention the interesting example of compensation of character or contradiction of character. For example, a sad brown might be enlivened by combination with a cheerful yellow, while a " strong, egotistical " purple overbears completely a " simpering, mild " blue. It is likely that this character aspect is inadequately grasped by many people in the combining of colours. For example, it would seem that some women in choosing dress colour schemes, whilst very sensitive to the clashing or blending of colours as such, ignore the more subtle beauty which is derived from a blending of this æsthetic character of the colours with their own characters and temperaments.

These experiments did not confirm the supposition that complementary colours * make the most pleasing combinations, as has been asserted by some. Further, it was found that, where such preferences did occur, it was largely among the subjects of a lower æsthetic type, very rarely among the character type. Of

---

* Complementary colours are those which when combined give white—*e.g.* red and green, or blue and yellow. It should be noted that the light of different colours has to be mixed, not the pigments.

course complementary colours strengthen one other by contrast, so that no doubt a combination of complementary colours will be pleasing where this is desired, for example where the tints are somewhat faint. Certainly it has been found by several experimenters that colours that are too much alike are often disliked in combination. There seems to be almost an intellectual difficulty in thinking of them apart. Further, those who are especially fond of intense colours—children, for example—may prefer a combination of complementary colours because they intensify one another by contrast.

Experiments with seventy-five children between the ages of nine and seventeen showed that such combinations were very popular with them, though they were even fonder of having together those colours which adjoin one another in the spectrum—thus: red, orange, yellow, green, blue, and purple.

I have devoted a considerable amount of space to the discussion of the " types " of colour perception, partly because of their own interest, and partly because similar mental attitudes seem to be found throughout the whole field of æsthetics. Thus they appear, as we shall see, in the appreciation of pictures and of music.

The present writer performed a series of **experiments with combinations of three colours.** Coloured wools of many tints such as are used for testing colour blindness were used. I selected groups of three colours, pretty much at haphazard, simply avoiding a too frequent selection of wools of very similar shades. The skeins of wool were about eight inches long and three quarters of an inch thick. Subjects were asked to arrange them vertically thus ||| in the way which they found most pleasing. They were afterwards asked to arrange the wools in

the most pleasing manner horizontally thus ===. I
had in view not the somewhat barren problem as to
what colours "go together," but what principles
underlie the grouping of such colours.

Naturally, the principle of weight already mentioned appeared in *the horizontal arrangement*, the
heaviest (*i.e.* darkest) colour being placed at the
bottom, then the next darkest, and the lightest
colour on the top. But sometimes this principle was
quite overthrown by others. Thus it might be sacri-
ficed in order to separate two colours which looked
particularly bad together, or it might be said that
two of the colours went together too well to be sepa-
rated, in spite of the lack of balance. Or, again,
a bad colour, though the heaviest, might be placed
in the middle to "tone it down." Another subject
placed the worst colour in the middle because she
"naturally looked more at the top and bottom."
Further, it seems possible for a lack of balance to be
felt if the two heaviest colours are beneath the lightest,
so that once or twice the lightest was placed in the
middle, lest the base of the triad should look too
heavy.

As to *the vertical arrangement*, most of these same
principles may be at work. The principle most comparable with that of weight is that of balance, in accordance with which one light colour would be placed
between two dark and heavy ones, or the most "pro-
found" and solid colour would go in the centre.

A curious emphasis of the right or left side occasionally evinced itself. This led to various complications. Thus, some subjects would place the colour
they liked best on the left, others on the right, as
being the most prominent position according to their
judgment. Others, again, would place their favourite
colour in the centre for a similar reason. People have
also been found who, in the case of pictures, like to

have the interesting things on the left (or right). Some subjects seem to " read " the colours from left to right, others (few in number) from right to left. Hence one subject liked her favourite colour to be on the right because the other " led up to it." On the other hand, one subject arranged the colours as follows : crimson—fawn—blue, adding, " I naturally read from left to right, and if this blue were at the left it would be impossible to get rid of it before passing to the two others, because of its aggressive qualities." Again, a subject arranged three other colours thus : crimson—green—pale green, adding, " I want to get rid of the disagreeable crimson, and I lose it first if I put it on the left as I read from left to right. It seems to suggest leaving a hot, stuffy room and getting out into the open."

Those who read the colours from one side to the other naturally sometimes base their plan of arrangement upon the principle of " pleasant transition," A leading on to B and B to C ; or again, we may have the triad really divided into two largely independent pairs, AB and BC, and the colours are arranged then according to the principles that govern the pairing of colours. With one subject one unpleasant colour was practically ignored, and put on the outside, " because it does not interfere with the others so much in that position." In contrast with such unsympathetic treatment was the attitude of another subject, who put a certain colour in the centre " because it was too delicate to be on the outside."

In two cases associations with nature seemed to determine the position of the colours. Thus the arrangement $\left\{\begin{array}{l}\text{blue}\\ \text{pale green}\\ \text{brown}\end{array}\right\}$ was liked because it resembled the dark colour of a ploughed field with green foliage and the blue sky above. But, on the whole, associations were very rare in these experiments with three colours, much rarer than in experiments with single colours. This is not surprising in view of the greater complexity of the group of three.

Once more, in studying the results contributed by many subjects, one is impressed with the extraordinary variety of reasons for liking or disliking certain colour groups which may be given by different individuals. An ideal group no doubt would be one that was in accord with all the various principles in so far as this is possible. Some, however, will obviously conflict with others.

In such experiments as these we are, as we have said, only touching the simple elements which go to build up the beautiful. When our colours are the colours of material objects of daily use, further complications will enter in—for example, the suitability to the purpose of the object. The reader could easily entertain himself by obtaining judgments from different people about the arrangement of a vase of various coloured flowers, or the colour scheme of a room as depicted in advertisements of furnishers or on the colours of a fashion-plate. But he will find that interesting results will only be obtained in so far as he is able to get *reasons* for the judgments of his subjects.

In concluding the chapters on colour, we may add that, great as its influence is in the pictorial and decorative arts, the immediate effect of individual colours is modified as soon as it enters as an element into such a complicated object as a picture. The significance and meaning of the colour here take part of our attention. If the reader will turn a coloured picture upside down, he will note how strikingly the colours stand out, some perhaps which he had never noted before being occupied more with the objects they represented. Similar results may be observed by looking at a landscape as one lies upon the ground.

Even in music sounds probably appeal to us less as sounds when they have meaning, as in the words of a song, though of course the total effect may be greater because of the added significance of the words. For the purest and strongest impressions of the beauty of sound itself we turn to instrumental music. And thus we get developments of the various arts by each selecting one aspect of beauty which it shall specially represent, statuary or black and white etchings giving us form without colour, while the beauty of colour without any significant form is at least represented by the modern tendency to self-toned wall-papers. Music has developed one-sidedly with some primitive peoples, in the direction of highly elaborate rhythm, to which the music owes almost all its effect, there being little melody and practically no harmony.

One visionary did indeed suggest that we might have a music of colours as we have a music of sounds, if we could invent an instrument for giving us a stream of different colours in constantly varying but harmonious combinations; and doubtless the power of colour is adequate for this if the mechanical means were not so much harder to devise than it has proved in the case of sounds.*

* Since these words were written a " colour-organ " has actually been exhibited.

CHAPTER IV.

THE BEAUTY OF FORM.

WE have seen that mere patches of colour, of no significant shape, may be in themselves highly pleasing. For *full* æsthetic enjoyment, however, it is not enough, of course, that the eye should be stimulated by beautiful colours. The beauty of form must be added too, just as pleasing musical tones and chords must be arranged into various rhythms and orders if the highest beauty of music is to be realised. Further, shape and form may be found pleasing apart from colour—indeed with the very minimum of

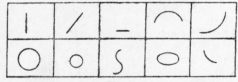

Fig. 2.

material, such as plain black lines on a white background, just as, again, we may find pleasure in rhythms made by the mere tapping of a pencil on a table.

One of the most interesting and surprising things which experiments have revealed, is the fact that people can find themselves markedly pleased or displeased even with simple lines and curves, often much to their own astonishment. A long series of experiments was performed by Professor L. J. Martin with about fifty figures such as those given in Fig. 2. As

will be seen, these include a number of straight lines
of different lengths, some curves, circles, and an
ellipse, some of the lines being thicker than the others.
The long lines were about five inches long, the short
ones about half that length.

Each of these lines was drawn upon a separate
card, and these were presented in turn to eight persons, who were asked to state whether they liked the
line or disliked it, or merely found it indifferent.
The cards were also presented two at a time, the
subjects being asked which they preferred. In this
way each card was compared with each of the others.
Now although such simple materials were being used,
only one out of eight subjects found all the lines
"indifferent." The others discovered that they had
very emphatic preferences, and several afterwards
expressed their surprise at the definite feelings of like
or dislike they felt towards the lines, one of them
saying that she had "nearly as strong a liking for
her favourite lines as for her favourite pictures."
Probably these likes and dislikes were stimulated by
the *comparison* of the lines. But in many cases the
method of comparison only serves to bring to consciousness a reason for preference which was not
thought of before, though present nevertheless. It
is sometimes only when we come to contrast Mr. B
with Mr. A that we realise what it is in A that
attracts us—something which is only brought home
to us by its marked absence in B, or by the presence
of the opposite.

Simple as the materials may be, we find that the
reasons for liking or disliking them may be very
varied. They vary greatly with the individual, and
the reasons may be in themselves very simple or
complex. Thus, so apparently simple a fact as the
position of one card compared with the other affects
its power of giving pleasure. Thus A may be pre-

ferred to B when it is on the right of B, but not
when it is on the left. A careful experimenter will
allow for this (which is called the "space error"),
and, whatever the objects may be, will present each
pair twice, first with A to the right and B to the left,
and later, probably at some subsequent sitting, with
B to the right and A to the left. It is easy to understand why a pair of lines should be more pleasing
as a pair when arranged in one way rather than
another : the figure suggested by the combination
of the two may be more symmetrical in one position
than in another. But the reason why preference for
one over the other is reversed when the position is
reversed is more difficult to explain. We shall meet
with a possible explanation on p. 44.

The *size* of the lines and circles also affects the
extent to which they please us. Generally the larger
lines and arcs mentioned above were preferred to the
smaller, and so were the larger circles—a result which,
Miss Martin remarks, conflicts with Burke's statement that smallness enhances beauty. Of course the
size of any kind of line or figure which is most pleasing depends partly upon the distance from which it
is viewed. Individuals vary here again. Some do
prefer the very small, just as some persons find
miniatures most attractive, while others admire
especially pictures large enough to cover the wall of
a fair-sized room. It was found, too, that the subjects varied as to which *width* of line they preferred,
most but not all preferring the broad lines to the
narrower. Naturally, the longer a line is the greater
width it can carry without looking disproportioned,
until indeed we reach the stage at which a short line
is so wide that we begin to regard it as a rectangle,
when our whole attitude changes. One subject I
tested with a thin line thus ——— which was found
indifferent ; the line was then thickened somewhat,

and was found pleasing, because "more powerful";
the first line, my subject remarked, looked too much
like a minus sign. The line was further thickened,
and was found less pleasing, and eventually displeasing, "clumsy," the subject remarking that I
need not go on widening it any more, as she was
sure she would not like it again. However, I continued to widen the line, and suddenly, when the
line was over a quarter of an inch thick, my subject
discovered that it was pleasing again, because it was
beginning to look, for a moment, like a rectangle,
though perhaps again appearing momentarily as a line.

This simple illustration of a sudden and entire
change of mental attitude towards an object is typical
of many cases in all departments of æsthetics. Thus
one of my students disliked a greenish colour when
she saw it as a greeny yellow, but liked it when
she regarded it as a very faded brown-green, such as
one sees often on autumn leaves. Another student,
on hearing a chord, found it highly interesting and
pleasing. Then it suddenly occurred to him that it
was a discord, and immediately it appeared somewhat
displeasing.

Similarly, a line such as / has been found to be

displeasing when regarded as a bad vertical, but pleasing when regarded as a horizontal which is raising
itself to the vertical. Or again, the same subject
may dislike a line as a bad vertical one day, and on
a subsequent day may like it when apprehended as
an arrow which is being shot upwards. Similar mental somersaults may be met with in other sections
of our study—for example in music, where a "neutral" third may be heard sometimes as a major
third, sometimes as a minor third.

In view of the marked influence of the mental
attitude upon our appreciation of such simple

materials (which are, however, the raw material of pictorial and musical art), one may wonder what the effect will be when many such items are grouped together into one picture or one piece of music. But it will be seen that in these more complex structures the meaning of each item is largely determined for the observer by the whole. It is not open to me to regard a patch of colour as an autumn leaf and so pleasing, when it obviously represents a particularly bad cloud. Our apprehension of a colour or a line is generally determined by the context. Thus the more complex an object is, the less do such individual differences of apprehension enter, as far as the items themselves are concerned. Yet differences of training, temperament, experience, and mood, &c., still affect enormously our appreciation of the picture or piece of music as a whole, as we shall see. Further, the charm, or at least the wide popularity, of some works of art seems to be in their indefiniteness, in their very capability of suiting many minds and many moods.

We saw in the case of colours how important a part *associations* play in determining our pleasure or displeasure. The same has been observed in reference to lines. One subject of Professor Martin based his judgment entirely on associations, one circle being liked because it was about the size and shape of a certain picture, or a vertical line resembled a " pussy-willow branch," and an oblique line recalled " a road between pine trees."

Sometimes the subjects reported that they liked or disliked the combination—*i.e.* figure—formed by the two lines which were being compared, and that this affected their judgment on the individual lines. Exactly the same thing has been observed by the present writer in experiments upon pictures and upon musical chords. Thus picture A (or chord A) may appear pleasing by itself, and picture B (or chord B) displeasing or indifferent by itself. Yet when the two came to be compared, B is preferred to A—to the surprise, often, of the person judging. It would appear that the whole formed by the pair produces in us some mood or mental attitude more favourable to B than the mood in which B was previously judged, so that this phenomenon is probably another curious example of the effect of different modes of apprehension of which we have just been speaking.

It must not be supposed that subjects are always able to give a reason for their likes or dislikes of simple lines and figures. In the majority of cases the opposite is the fact. But one kind of reason is of special interest, and may be discussed in some detail.

The influence of movement or suggested movement in our appreciation of lines. — Professor Martin found that a subject spoke of the pleasure a line gave him " because he felt himself drawing it." " This led me," says Professor Martin, " to examine the results with a view to finding, if possible, the part played by the imitative movements of the hand and arm in the æsthetic impression. I reasoned that if such imitative movements occurred they would be along the lines of least resistance—in short, that lines easiest to draw would be most liked. My own introspections, the fact that many persons whom I had asked to draw an oblique line drew the right oblique, and certain statements made by McAllister, as that the slant in a " back hand " writing required movements that are comparatively very hard to make, led me to believe that the left oblique would be harder to draw, and that therefore, if the imitative movements just referred to played a determinative rôle, the left oblique would be less liked."

But it was not found that the left oblique was less

liked than the right.   The votes were almost equal.
Possibly Professor Martin overestimates the difficulty
of drawing the left oblique \ compared with the
right /. If one places the hand somewhat above the
line or well to its right, as schoolboys often do in
writing and drawing, it seems to me to be at least
as easy to draw a left as a right oblique, if not easier.
And it must be remembered that many people,
especially women, habitually write " back hand."
Further, it is interesting to note that the line 2
was preferred to S by all subjects but one, and
the former will probably be more easily drawn by the
majority of people. A more conclusive argument,
however, was drawn from further experiments.   One
hundred students were asked to draw the human profile.   Eighty-eight drew the profile facing to the left
(as it is generally drawn by children and in the art of
primitive peoples).   Now, though undoubtedly those
students would find it easier to draw the profile thus
(facing to the left), *yet they did not show a preference
for profiles facing to the left* as compared with those
facing to the right. Fifty of them were shown a
transparent slide on which the profile could be faced
right or left by reversing the slide.   Twenty-five
students preferred it facing to the left, fifteen to the
right, and ten had no choice.

Nor is it found that modern artists have any preference for profiles facing to the left.   Fifty-three
volumes of the *Masters in Art* series of illustrated
monographs were examined, the pictures being
divided into four classes—single portraits, pictures
of the Madonna and Child, other pictures with only
two figures, and pictures with more than two figures.

The number of figures facing right and left were counted, but no appreciable superiority in numbers was found for the left profile in any of the four classes. Yet it is argued reasonably that artists would probably be alive to any condition which was likely to help them in producing a pleasing effect, both to themselves and to others.

The Influence of Eye-movement.—It is of course true that a human face is a complex object, and one that we judge not merely for its shape but for its expression. Hence any usual tendency to be influenced in our judgment of simple lines by the suggestion of easy movements, may be lost here in the more complex mental state involved in looking at a portrait, as compared with a straight line or curve. What then, it may be asked, occurs when simple lines and figures are looked at ? More especially may not the *movement of the eyes* influence our pleasure in looking at lines ? Now the muscles of the eye are so placed that one might expect a kind of side pull. The three pairs of muscles of each eye are not arranged quite symmetrically. Hence, it has been argued, the eye moves more naturally and easily in a curve, and therefore we find greater pleasure in looking at curves than in looking at straight lines. This argument sounds very plausible, but the facts are entirely against it. In the first place, curves are by no means so universally preferred as might be expected, and as, indeed, Ruskin dogmatically asserted. For example, in Martin's research, if the various figures are arranged in classes (straight lines, circles, arcs, &c.) and then placed in order of pleasingness for each person, we find that all subjects except one preferred the straight lines to the arcs of circles, and three out of eight prefer the straight lines even to the circles also. The average order of popularity is as follows : first, circles, then straight lines, waving lines, the ellipse, and last the arcs of circles. One subject indeed disliked the circle because the eye "seemed to go round and round," and this was found unpleasant.

A second argument against this eye-movement theory lies in the fact that we are remarkably insensitive to eye-movements themselves. We know when our eyes move in the case of slight movements largely from the fact that the point of central vision moves across seen objects. But in the dark it is often difficult to say when our eyes move. If the reader watches the recurrent flash of a lighthouse on a dark night, and tries to keep his eyes fixed upon a point where the light last appeared, he will often

Fig. 3.   Fig. 4.

find, when the flash recurs, that his eyes have wandered some distance from the point without his knowing it. Yet if the movement of our eyes is to account for our disliking a line which has a very slight irregularity in it, we ought to be extraordinarily sensitive to the slightest movement of the eye.

A still more conclusive argument is found in experiments performed by two independent investigators. Subjects were instructed to look at a curve, and meanwhile photographic impressions of the movements of the eye were taken by means of a camera so placed as to catch the image of a small light reflected by the front surface of the eye as it moved. It was found that the eye does not follow the line of a pleasing curve, such as that in Fig. 3. On the contrary, the eye moves in jerks as shown in Fig. 4, and the movements carried out in looking at an ugly variation of Fig. 3 were practically the same as those shown in Fig. 4. Similarly it has been shown that, when looking at a vase as shown in Fig. 5, the eye moves in an irregular way, such as is indicated by the dotted lines.

We may take it as fairly certain, then, that our pleasure in looking at lines and figures is not due to the actual sensations due to the movement of the eyes. Indeed we can take in the beauty of a line or figure without *any* movement of the eye.

The Influence of Suggested Movement.—It seems

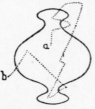

possible, however, that pleasure may be found in the *suggestion* of movement by a line, if that suggestion is of the right kind. Now graceful movements are generally associated with ease, regular movements are more effi- cient as a rule than jerky, irreg- ular ones, and so the suggestion of such easy, regular movements

Fig. 5.

would be pleasant. But as regards the pleasure in suggested movement, the mind is more subtle and more sensitive than the muscular system by which movements are made. For angles and ugly bends may be displeasing to look upon even when the movements involved in tracing them with the finger are not appreciably unpleasant ; or lines, in making which distinctly pleasant movements are involved, may appear much less pleasing, or even displeasing to the eye. This was very clearly shown in some very simple experiments carried out by the present writer. Sixteen subjects were asked to close their eyes and draw with free-and-easy move- ments of the hand and arm simple curves and figures, such as spirals and intermingled curves, on paper, and after each drawing to jot down, without opening the eyes, whether the movement had been pleasing, displeasing, indifferent, very or slightly pleasing, and so on. When five drawings had been made the subjects looked at their figures and expressed judgment as to their *visual appearance*, again describing them as pleasing, displeasing, &c. Marks were awarded to the various figures according to the judgments, very pleasing scoring 3, pleasing 2, slightly pleasing 1, indifferent 0, slightly displeasing – 1, displeasing – 2, very displeasing – 3. It was found that in the case of every subject except one, the appearances of the lines had scored much less than the movements which executed them, the total scores being : lines as judged by movement, 172 ; as judged by appearance, 99. The subject who was the exception to the rule had made his figures very small, confining himself practically to finger movements.

I also performed some experiments with curves cut out of cardboard. The subject was asked to close his eyes, and to trace these curves with his fingers, and state whether they felt pleasing or displeasing. The general result was that, whilst awkward angles were felt as distinctly unpleasant, there was not such sensitivity to small irregularities as was shown when the cards were looked at.

Yet even these small irregularities, not felt through touch, or the movement of the hand, may to the sight be *representative* of what has meant unpleasant movement. An angle drawn on a very small scale may be *of the same type* as a larger corner and may suggest the unpleasantness of the latter.

Thus, though the mind has learned much through movement, *the mind itself progresses beyond the point to which its instructor, movement, leads it.* We learn through movement the pleasantness of even, graceful movements, and then we refine upon these. The mind sets up an ideal of movement even beyond any known in its own experience, just as the sculptor may imagine forms more beautiful than the deftness of his hand can devise. A further analogy of this advance of the mind beyond its practical experience may be found in the case of the geometrician, who thinks, in his axioms and definitions, of lines and circles more perfect than any he can construct or has ever seen constructed ; and also, to go further afield, in the case of the moralist who sets up ideals of conduct beyond his own attainments or those of anyone else.

It may be that such suggestions of movement as we are speaking of need only be very vague even when they are a source of pleasure to us. For a feeling of pleasure or displeasure may arise even when the idea or experience which originally caused it is only sub-conscious, or even when we are unable to trace the source of the pleasure or to remember its original cause. For example, we may receive an agreeable piece of news, or think of some pleasant plan which we can carry out ; and then it sometimes happens that, shortly after, the feeling of pleasure " comes over us again "—though we forget for the moment what it was that caused us pleasure. And it is probably in this unconscious or sub-conscious way, as a rule, that the suggestions of agreeable movements enter into our mind and contribute to its pleasure. (It is interesting to note here, too, that when figures, pictures, or words are exposed on a card for a mere second or two, it is found that we may experience a feeling of pleasure or displeasure even before we get a clear idea as to what the figure or picture is—a feeling, too, which is afterwards seen to have its own ground in the nature of the figure presented.)

The Pleasure of Successful Mental Activity.—
Our pleasure in straight lines or regular curves or
symmetrical figures is not, however, entirely to be
explained by the suggestion of
pleasant movement. We must
fall back on a fundamental principle of psychology, that *mental
activity is pleasant in so far as it
is successful.* Now attention is a form of mental
activity, and we find that we experience pleasure
when the attention process is facilitated by the
unity of the object. A conglomeration of lines
having no regular plan about them gives us no
pleasure. A line such as that in Fig. 6 displeases us.
Having set out to be a curve, with a certain regularity
about it, it ceases to follow this plan. Our attention
is thwarted and disappointed. The line cannot be
taken in at a glance as a unity, as it could if the
even curve had continued. Of course *some*
baffling of mental effort may be the means
of stimulating to keener activity, and if
this is successful it may be the means of
further pleasure. Too simple a line or
figure does not provide us with enough
about which to occupy our mind. But a
serpentine curve, while changing, changes
gradually; there is not the same " shock "
about the change. We may even like a
very sudden change in some of the lines of
a figure, if the figure as a whole is enough
to occupy fully this heightened activity of
mind, and if the figure as a whole can be
apprehended with comparative ease. Thus
starting from A in Fig. 7, we get a great
change in direction at B and again at C. But we
have now a more complex figure than a straight
line. And the principle of change is grasped at once.

Fig. 6.

Fig. 7.

Indeed the plan of the whole line is taken in at once at the first glance, before any unpleasant feeling can arise. The object of attention in which we must not be disappointed is, practically from the first, not the direction of the line A—B or B—C, but the regularity of the sizes of the lines and angles.

In a complex design also, in masses of architecture, or in music, many surprises in the way of side excursions and diversions are permissible, and will add to the mental excitement and pleasure, provided that the main stream of attention to the whole is not seriously diverted, and provided that these diversions can themselves be fitted eventually into the main scheme of the whole.

This principle of the dependence of æsthetic enjoyment upon the satisfaction of attention will become clearer, and its importance be realised more fully, when we come to consider the æsthetic appreciation of pictures in subsequent chapters.

Æsthetic Illusions of Form.—We have observed that lines may suggest movement to us. Theoretically this may be done in two ways. (1) The lines may suggest a movement *of ours* in the direction indicated by the line, or a movement of ours *with* the line. This is the kind of suggestion of which we have spoken chiefly so far. (2) The lines *themselves* may appear to us as about to move or as trying to move. In other words, they may seem to embody an activity in themselves, an activity which we, as active beings, read into them. This is but one example of a general tendency of the human imagination, which, as Ruskin says, "rejoicing in its own excessive life, puts gesture into clouds, and joy into waves, and voices into rocks." *

* Psychologically these two kinds of suggested movement are closely bound up with one another. The point is too abstruse for a book of this nature. We will only add, that the point of connection is to be found in the phrase " which we, as active beings, read into " the lines.

According to Lipps, a distinguished German psychologist, we cannot get away from this tendency to "feel into" a line this active power. The vertical line seems to strive upwards, the curve bends itself.

The standing rectangle ▯ holds itself in and so gets power to stand up. The lying rectangle ▭ stretches itself out or lets itself go. It has been suggested that we should call this "feeling into" a line

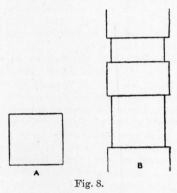

Fig. 8.

or figure Empathy, a parallel word to Sympathy, "feeling with." Lipps explains many optical illusions of form by reference to this empathy. Fig. 8 gives an example. The square in B is really the same size as A, but it appears taller, says Lipps, because the heavier figure B raises itself up more vigorously against gravity than does figure A, and the enclosed square in B shares in this. The weight of the figures above in B apparently emphasises the activity of the vertical lines of the square in their resistance to gravity. This greater activity of the vertical lines in the square in B is translated into greater apparent size, so that the square in B looks taller than A.

I tested eighty subjects with the above figures. Sixty per cent. agreed with Lipps in finding the enclosed square in B taller than A, but twenty per cent. found them equal in height, and twenty per cent. actually asserted that A appeared the taller. Of seventy-one children between the ages of eight and fifteen, only twenty-four per cent. did not experience the illusion. It is evident, then, that this æsthetic illusion, though not universal, is quite common, and its greater frequency among the children indicates that it is of a somewhat fundamental nature. Some adults doubtless escaped the illusion by concentrating their attention very carefully upon the *square* in B, ignoring the superimposed structure.

If the æsthetic interpretation of the illusion is correct, there is little doubt that similar illusions will frequently occur in architecture and in pictures of buildings supported by pillars. The activity " felt into " the supporting columns will, for many, make them appear taller than they really are. Those who had the opposite illusion in Fig. 8 (*under*-estimating the enclosed square) may represent another class who find that the superimposed weights act as a depressant, crushing down the supporting pillar. It is conceivable, indeed, that with some the nature of the illusion depends upon the proportion of the apparent strength of the column to the apparent weight of the superstructure, the columns appearing to be pressed down when the weight appears disproportionately heavy.

To some people the vertical lines at the top of Fig. 8 appear to converge. Lipps suggests that this is because the outward spreading tendency of the oblong below carries the lower end of these vertical lines along with it, the free ends appearing to approach one another again. This recalls the illusion which sometimes occurs in architectural columns, which seem to get narrower towards the middle of the column, and then to widen out again, a tendency which was sometimes counteracted in Greek buildings by making the column actually to bulge outwards in the centre. The raising of the central portion of the stylobate (the unbroken pedestal upon which a row of columns stood) in Doric architecture would seem to have been done in order to counteract any illusion of "sagging" in the middle, but such an illusion does not seem explicable upon the principles expounded by Lipps.

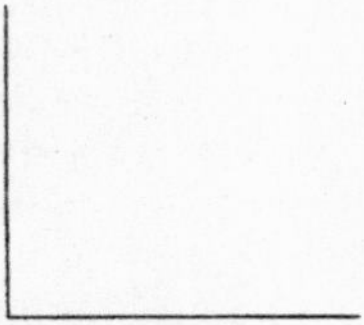

[Many other illusions of form are explained by Lipps by the principle of the "inner activity" of

Fig. 9.

lines. One or two of the illusions, however, thus explained by Lipps have been shown to be due probably to other causes. For example, a square appears to most people taller than it is broad. This apparent over-estimation of the vertical line as compared with the horizontal, as in Fig. 9, was explained by Lipps similarly to the illusion of Fig. 8. Some experiments, however, made by the present writer suggest that it is due to physiological rather than psychological causes; for it was found that some persons have a much greater illusion with Fig. 9 with one eye, used alone, than with the other— three times as great in the case of two subjects. Yet training in drawing enables one to overcome the illusion, and it was found that it decreased very considerably with children who were receiving instruction in drawing.]

CHAPTER V.

BALANCE AND SYMMETRY.

IN one of the earliest experiments in æsthetics, Fechner, who may be called the founder of this branch of experimental psychology, tried to find what proportions of length to breadth made the most pleasing rectangle. He offered ten rectangles for his subjects to choose from. These varied from a square to an oblong with sides in the proportion of five to two. Over 300 men and women were tested. The most popular, both with men and women, was the rectangle here given. It scored about thirty-five per cent. of the preferences. Now the peculiarity of this rectangle is that its sides correspond to the "golden section" of a line. This we get by dividing a line so that the whole line bears to the greater part the same ratio that the greater part bears to the lesser part. The pleasingness of the "golden section" has been explained in accordance with the principle of facilitation of attention, which we explained in the last chapter. Thus it is held that the mental transition from attention to the whole line to attention to the greater part prepares us for the further transition to the smaller part, because the step is proportionately the same.

It is conceivable that some similar explanation may account for the popularity of the rectangle given above, though it is hard to see why the two sides should be subconsciously added together to form a whole. Furthermore, more recent experi-

Fig. 10.

ments have discredited the supposed popularity of the golden section of a line. Nine subjects were asked to divide a line in the way that appeared most pleasing to them. Each subject made in all seventy-two judgments. The " line " consisted of an illuminated slit 160 mm. long, which the subject could divide as he pleased by moving along the line a strip of steel by means of strings. Only in the case of two subjects did the most pleasing line prove to be very near the golden section. The rest preferred divisions of the line differing markedly from the golden section. Furthermore, it was shown how misleading it may be to *average* the measurements of lines, &c., judged most pleasing. If green were found to be the most popular colour with half the subjects tested, and blue the most popular with the remaining subjects, it would obviously be wrong to say that blue-green was the most popular colour. It is scarcely less inaccurate to average pleasing proportions of lines. Thus a square and a very narrow oblong might each prove very pleasing to different groups of individuals, but if the average of such figures gave the golden section rectangle, we could not infer that this last was the most pleasing on the average. This method of averaging seems to be responsible for some of the credit given to the golden section of a line. In the experiments on line division just mentioned it was found that no one division could rightly be said to be the most pleasing, as individuals varied so enormously, and also to most of them there were two or more divisions of the line which appeared equally pleasing, and one or other of which they generally adopted. Yet when the *average* of all the various divisions was taken it proved to be almost exactly the same as the golden section. But to state this as the most pleasing division on the average would obviously be misleading. For, as we have said, the actual (or approximate) proportions of the golden section were scarcely ever adopted.

Three rough generalisations, however, seem to be possible from these tests. The smaller part of the line was rarely made less than one quarter of the whole ; a slight remove from the centre was almost invariably disagreeable ; and division at the centre was not frequent.

The introspective remarks of the subjects indicate that even with an unequal division the line is felt to be in a sense symmetrical. The short part has greater importance given to it by a concentration of interest, or " the long line means an effortless activity, the short a more strenuous activity." Or again, " the short part looks wider, brighter, and more important than the long." Here added interest and attention are apparently causing even some degree of illusion as to the brightness of the short part of the line. This recalls the illusion mentioned previously (p. 25), in which a colour appeared brighter when it was in a more prominent position.

Thus any impression of inequality of weight is quite lost through added meaning, indeed none of the subjects were troubled with a feeling of inequality of weight.

When part of the line was replaced by a more or less complex pattern it was found that the patterned part was almost invariably made the shorter part. Here, again, greater interest and importance balanced greater size.

It is interesting to compare these experiments with others carried out by Miss E. D. Puffer. Her experiments were planned to find the principles underlying the symmetrical arrangement of lines and figures in pictures. Her subjects were confronted with an oblong board, covered with black cloth. On this a narrow strip of white cardboard (8 cm. by 1 cm.) was placed, in different positions on different occasions. The subject was then asked to place a strip just twice the length of the other, in the position which gave the most pleasing effect, as, for example, in Fig. 11. Now it was found that very often the arrangement could be interpreted as depending on mechanical balance, that is, the long line was placed roughly half as far from the centre as the short line, just as a heavy man must sit only half-way along one side of a seesaw beam to balance a boy only half his weight sitting at the other end of the seesaw.* But many arrangements could not possibly be explained on this principle. Indeed it is doubtful whether those arrangements which did follow this rule were really based upon any clear apprehension of the principle of mechanical balance. I tested one of my own subjects with a long ruler, balanced on a pencil. On one side of the fulcrum I placed a strip of cardboard 10 cm. long, and, holding the ruler steady meanwhile, I asked my subject to place on the ruler a strip only half the size of the other, in such a position that the ruler would be evenly balanced. In every case the subject (a very intelligent one) actually placed the short strip *nearer* to the centre of the ruler, quite contrary to the principle of mechanical balance. Similarly, when I placed the short strip on the ruler and asked her to balance it with the long strip, she disobeyed the law of balance. Yet when I gave her a test similar to Miss Puffer's,

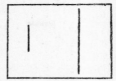

Fig. 11.

* Another investigator found that light colours had to be placed further from the centre than darker " heavier " colours on the other side of a central line, in order to obtain a feeling of balance.

she at once placed the short strip about twice as far on one side of the central line as the long strip was on the other, and then recognised forthwith that she had been wrong all the time with the ruler tests. The error was not due to mere careless haste, for the subject, in doing the ruler tests, had deliberately thought about the balance of a seesaw. The point of interest is that, in this case at least, the æsthetic sense of balance was far more certain than the know-ledge concerning mechanical balance, and could scarcely be said to be based upon it.

However, granting that the feeling of mechanical

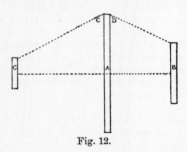

Fig. 12.

balance is of influence in some cases, it could not, as we said, explain many of the arrangements of the lines. A subsequent investigator, working with three lines arranged somewhat as in Fig. 12 (A being the fixed centre line), found that often the line B was so placed by subjects that the angle b was equal to the angle c, and that subjects were conscious of this principle of arrangement.

But this cannot explain Miss Puffer's results, as in most of her experiments she did not use any centre line.

She herself contends that *the principle which con-*

flicts sometimes with that of mechanical balance is the demand for the filling of the whole space without large gaps.

The subjects were obviously aware of this desire. They wanted " to take in the whole field," or " not to be disturbed by too large a black space in the centre." Thus, even when the large line was near one end of the oblong, the small line would sometimes be placed near the centre, and thus it would avoid the necessity of a wide empty space in the centre of the board. At the same time the central position of the small line would give it greater importance, and so enable it to balance the long line more adequately. Thus the principle of mechanical balance may not be entirely absent even in this case.

The Influence of Suggested Movement.—Further experiments dealt with the influence of suggested movement. In a picture, movement may be suggested in two ways : (1) by the direction of lines, for example the upward movement suggested by the converging lines of a church spire ; and (2) by the representation of a moving body, as, for example, a bird on the wing or a galloping horse. Ex-

Fig. 13.

periments were devised similar to those just described, in which movement was suggested by using pointed strips of cardboard and sloping them, as in Fig. 13. It was found that a line pointing as in Fig. 13 suggested a movement inwards, and that this was said to make it lighter—*i.e.* the line B would " balance " the bigger line at A better if A were pointed inwards, than if A were vertical ; for A seems to be moving inwards, and it appears that the impression is almost the same as though the movement were already accomplished and the line A already nearer the centre.

On the other hand, if A turns outwards as in Fig. 14, A is made " heavier," for it is as though it were already moved farther to the left, and so it can balance an equally large line B farther from the centre than A is.

But Miss Puffer's subjects also felt that these

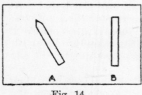

Fig. 14.

sloping lines gave the suggestion of the filling of the space over which movement was suggested, thus lessening the disagreeableness of large unfilled spaces. So that the demand for the filling of space would account for these arrangements

of sloping lines as well as would the principle of mechanical balance.

The Effect of Interest on Symmetry.—This was tested in a very simple but ingenious way. A small outline picture was placed on one side of the centre of the board, and a plain white square of the same size on the other side. The interest was kept up in the picture square by changing it every time a judgment was made. First the picture would be fixed in a certain position to the left of the board, and the subject was asked to arrange the paper square in the most pleasing position ; then the paper square would be fixed and the subject would have to place the picture, and so on. The results showed that an object that was interesting in itself, like a picture, acted as a " heavier " object than the plain square—*i.e.* it was placed nearer to the centre than the plain square. Of course, if the picture is vague and is put far out to start with, the interest in it as a picture may be very small, and it may thus act just as a plain square. But usually the effect of interest is most decided ; and it was shown again in further experiments, in which the plain square gave way to a postage stamp which remained the same throughout the tests, while the pictures were replaced by stamps which were changed for every new judgment, the interest in them thus being kept up. Here again the changed (and therefore interesting) stamp was generally placed nearer to the centre to balance the unchanged stamp placed farther out, as though the former were " heavier." It seems to me, however, that the natural tendency to have the more interesting object in a central position may often account, in part at least, for the placing of the picture or the changed stamp nearer the centre. It will be remembered that the desire to place well a favourite colour was shown very clearly in the reversal of the weight principle in the arrangement of colours. The heavier colour, if the more pleasing, would be placed at the apex of a triangle, above the lighter colour, because the apex was felt to be the more prominent and important position. It would seem likely that the same principle might hold in the arrangement of the interesting picture or stamp.

Further modifications of the experiments were adopted, bringing them still nearer to the conditions found in the case of pictures. Thus on one side was placed a picture of " the mouth of a railway tunnel closed tightly by an apparently massive door," whilst on the other side had to be balanced against it a picture of the same shape and size, and again representing a tunnel, but " showing the rails entering at a slight curve, the deep blackness within, and the small circle of light at the farther end." Or again, the pair of pictures would be (1) the gateway of a castle closed with iron doors with heraldic bearings, and

(2) the same gateway, but open, showing an open courtyard beyond. Thus in one of the two pictures the perspective effect of depth was obtained. Here the perspective picture was the more interesting, and, as in the stamp experiments, interest seemed to act as though it gave " weight." Certainly an evenly symmetrical arrangement was generally avoided.

Subjects frequently spoke of the difficulty of apprehending the two together, and as a rule the closed tunnel had little interest for them. Here again the desire to have the more interesting object in a more central position may have had more influence in determining its position than any feeling of mechanical balance. But the tendency towards the equal filling of space was also apparently at work, and there were often complications into which we have not space to enter here. We may simply add that Miss Puffer does not by any means interpret the principle of " mechanical balance " in a literal way, but suggests that any apparent heaviness of an object, in such experimental arrangements, is really a measure of its demand upon our attention. A large object and an interesting object are heavy for the same reason, because they call out the attention.

Symmetry in Pictures.—With the results of the foregoing experiments in mind, Miss Puffer examined 1000 good pictures with a view to finding to what extent there is balance or symmetry in pictures, in the sense of an equal distribution of attention to both sides of the central line. The pictures were taken from a collection of reproductions in black and white, the *Classiker Bilderschatz*, published by F. Bruchmann at Munich. The balance of the original picture would be partially determined by the arrangement of the colours, for a striking colour on one side would add weight to that side. Miss Puffer therefore examined a large number of the originals in

European galleries, but found that almost invariably
the balance was fairly represented in the black-and-
white reproductions. The pictures were divided into
groups according to their subjects—*e.g.* Madonna
and Child, Holy Family, Crucifixions, Allegorical,
Landscapes, Portraits, and so on. Now, in accordance with the principles exemplified by the preceding
experiment, " weight " is given to one side of the
picture by a specially interesting person or object,
by depth of perspective, or by direction of suggested
movement away from the centre. All these may
interplay in the balance of one picture. Thus, in the
case of the " Madonna Enthroned " (Raffaelino di
Francesco), the Child is on the right, facing straight
forward, the Madonna turns to the left, and also all
the saints but one are turning to the left, so that the
central interest in the Child is balanced against the
direction of the Madonna's attention and that of the
saints.

In the great portraits, the emphasis sometimes
given to one side by the turning of both the head and
body to that side is almost invariably balanced by
the direction of the glance coming backward, this last
being highly suggestive. Frequently the direction
of the look, or the massiveness of the main portion
of the body somewhat on one side of the picture, is
balanced by a small but highly interesting object
somewhat on the other side—often the hand, for
example, or a jewel, or elaborate embroidery. This is
especially characteristic of the portraits of Rembrandt
and Van Dyck. Such balancing by a variety of
elements in a picture adds greatly to the effect. A
slavish devotion to *geometrical* symmetry, on the
other hand, shown in a few pictures, gave a displeasing and even unbalanced effect, for the more subtle
" weight " of small but interesting objects had been
neglected.

In landscapes the main mass of objects on one side would be balanced by the depth of vista and sloping lines on the other, and the heavier the other side the deeper is the vista. In very few cases is the vista placed behind an attractive or noticeable part of the picture.

For a full description of the results from this patient investigation the reader must be referred to Miss Puffer's own writings. We have given sufficient here to show that the "balance" we demand in a picture is no mere geometrical symmetry, or equality of mass of the objects on either side, but that the more subtle influence of interest, and attention, and possibly of suggested movement, are predominant in giving the beauty of symmetry to a picture.

Such principles are doubtless chiefly of negative value to the artist, teaching him what to avoid. But in the composition of his picture the artist must have further positive reasons for placing his objects. Composition, according to Ruskin, may best be defined as " the help of everything in the picture by everything else "; and it is, he says, such a complex problem that there are but a few " elementary laws of arrangement traceable a little way." In painting, as in poetry, " mere fitting and adjustment of material is nothing—that is watchmaking," while " helpful and passionate harmony " is the outcome of " sacred invention."

As we have said, Miss Puffer attributes the weight or balancing power of an item in a picture to the extent to which it makes a call upon our attention. A picture is balanced and symmetrical when our attention is not called to one side more than to the other. Miss Puffer interprets expenditure of attention as " the measure of the motor impulses directed to the object of attention," and holds that, because our organism is a bilateral one (having a muscular system fairly evenly developed on both sides), we experience pleasure in a balanced picture, because it fulfils the demand of our system for " a set of reactions corresponding to the organism as a whole." But, apart from the very disputable identification of attention and motor impulses, it may be questioned whether we do not often find great enjoyment in muscular activities in which the respective sides of the body have very unequal shares. Another critic also suggests that we should expect, on Miss Puffer's theory, some discernible difference between right- and left-handed people as regards their perception of symmetry. We did indeed see, in the experiments with three colours, that some people show a strong desire to have the most pleasing or striking colour on one side, and that always, for them, the same side. But this was generally the left side, while left-handedness is, of course, exceptional. Something similar seems to occur with a few people as regards the arrangement of the interesting objects in a picture, but not to the extent we should expect if Miss Puffer's theory were adequate. At the same time Miss Puffer might argue that she only attempts to show, and *can* only attempt to show, a *general* balance of right and left, at least in pictures, not such an absolute equality as would be inconsistent with right- or left-handedness.

But the demand for a kind of **symmetry in a vertical direction** must also be kept in mind. Exact symmetrical divisions in a vertical direction, it is true, are not pleasing. " There is but one thoroughly ugly tower in Italy that I know of," wrote Ruskin, " and that is because it is divided into vertical equal parts—the tower of Pisa." But here comes in the weight principle which we found at work in the case of colours : we want the stronger and heavier below to support the lighter and weaker above. Let us consider, however, the case of a picture in which all the interesting objects are crowded at the bottom (or top) of the canvas, with a long stretch of uninteresting background (or foreground). Such a picture would obviously be unsatisfactory. But this is not explicable on the " bilateral theory " of Miss Puffer. Why, then, is it displeasing ? It cannot be merely that there is not *enough* to interest us, for the photographer who has taken too much uninteresting foreground into his picture may at once make the picture pleasing by cutting this foreground off and mounting only the top half, and the smaller picture thus made is not necessarily any less pleasing than one twice the size would be. The emptiness of a wall immediately surrounding a picture hung upon it does not displease us as would a wide empty space added on to the picture itself. This, I think, gives us a clue to a partial explanation at least of our objection to unbalanced pictures. The picture is offered as a *unity*, and must be apprehended as such. Even when, for the moment, our attention is concentrated on a small part of the picture, the eye is receiving impressions from surrounding parts, and our attention is, partially at least, given to these as well. In particular, such side impressions are preparing us to pass on to other objects or aspects of the picture, at least in the case of a good picture, where " everything is helped by everything else." Now the very inclusion of an empty space within the framework of a picture forces it upon our attention as part of the unity, but the supporting supplementary impressions expected are not there, unless, of course, the very emptiness of the space adds meaning and significance to the picture, as it may in a desert scene or a wide expanse of sea. We are not annoyed merely because the useless space comes within the range of vision, for so would the empty wall space if more of

the picture were cut off by means of a smaller frame.
But the wall does not *pretend* to be part of the picture.
The empty space within the frame does, and disap-
points us accordingly.

So far we have only spoken of the disagreeableness
of the empty space. But following a similar line of
thought it will be seen that the ideal arrangement of
a picture (from the point of view now under consideration) will be that in which, while we are concentrating attention on the central point of interest,
the maximum number of " helping " impressions are
received, and movement of the attention to other
points of interest, and back to the central point, is
facilitated. Assuming that the principal objects are
fairly central, then, if one side of the picture is lacking in its fair share of interest, the attention (necessarily drawn to it by visual impressions of that part
because it is a part of the whole which is being apprehended) will be disappointed, and many of the impulses of attention wasted ; indeed an effort will be
made to inhibit these. Thus there will be a marked
lessening of that restful absorption in the object
contemplated which characterises the true æsthetic
experience.

It seems probable, then, that the pleasure derived
from balance and symmetry may be referable, in part
at least, to that same principle of the easy satisfaction
of attention discussed in the preceding chapter.

CHAPTER VI.

EXPERIMENTS WITH PICTURES.

THE experimenter meets with serious difficulties when he tries to work with complex objects like pictures. The essential nature of experiment is that we should vary the conditions and trace the varying consequences to those varying conditions. Now it is comparatively easy to do this in the case of simple colours and figures. But to change one picture for another may be to introduce a host of differences ; and also the effect of a picture on a subject may be so complex that he himself may be misled in saying what elements in the picture appeal to him most. It is therefore not surprising that much still remains to be done in the way of experiments with pictures. A number of interesting investigations, however, have already been made.

It may be well to commence with experiments dealing with **the appreciation of pictures by school children.** We shall see that some of the points characteristic of the child's attitude towards pictures remain true even for some adults, especially for those of little general culture and education.

Obviously the first obstacle, in experimenting upon children with pictures, is the difficulty they find in explaining why they like or dislike a picture. It is certainly not fair to assume that they have not marked likings or dislikings for pictures merely because they are unable to give reasons for them. This is often true of adults even when a picture has a very decided attraction for them, or when it repels them, though in the latter case it is usually not so difficult to give a reason.

Further, even when children do give their reasons for liking a picture, there is a danger that they will repeat what they have heard about the pictures, or merely express ideas suggested to them by the pictures.

An interesting attempt to experiment on children, while avoiding the difficulty of introspection on their part, was made by Rudolf Schulze. He showed a number of pictures, one at a time, to a group of about a dozen German Elementary School girls between the ages of eleven and twelve. The children were told to close their eyes, and a picture was placed before the group. They were then told to open their eyes, and after a few seconds an instantaneous photograph was taken of the group, showing the expressions on their faces, produced by the picture. Of the thirteen pictures shown only two could be said to be peculiarly children's pictures. The others comprised pictures of the Crucifixion, several landscapes and figure pictures, including a Swiss village with snow-clad alps behind, a picture of Dawn, with soldiers sleeping, a sketch of tall trees waving in the wind, a lonely old couple walking in the moonlight, and so forth— pictures whose " mood " some might think would scarcely appeal to young children. But surprising results were obtained when the photos of the children were shown to an experienced teacher. Although he had no idea previously as to what pictures had been shown to the children, he was able to describe in every case the general type of picture at which the children had been looking when the photo was taken, and when he was shown the actual pictures used he was able to pair every picture with the photo that belonged to it. Another person only made two mistakes in fitting the pictures to their corresponding photos. These persons based their interpretations not only on the expressions on the faces of the children, but on the carriage of the head and of the body, and the hold-

ing of the hands, which lie loosely during the exposure
of restful pictures, but are often clenched when a more
stimulating picture is being looked at. Schulze also
gives very interesting photos illustrating the mimicry
shown in the facial expressions of the children.

He concludes that we can no longer say that children of this age do not understand landscape pictures,
and certainly the experiments are useful in counter-
balancing to some extent the *negative* results obtained
so often in asking children about their enjoyment of
such pictures. Of course one must not assume that
a certain expression upon a child's face means all
that a similar expression on the face of an adult does.
There are few kinds of facial expressions of which an
adult is capable which may not be shown on the face
even of an infant twelve months old. Yet while the
expressions shown in the photographs of these children may not signify as much as they would in the
case of adults, the fact that they were of the right
kind suggests that the children's mood was suited to
the apparent meaning of the picture—in other words,
that they understood the picture more or less as the
artist meant it to be understood.

Many observers agree that when young children,
say from six or seven to nine or ten years of age, are
asked why they like pictures, they refer entirely to
the contents of the pictures—that is, the individual
objects represented in them. The form and composition of the picture do not appeal to them; at
least they are not conscious of its influence. Their
reasons for liking a picture often tend to be mere
enumerations of objects represented in the picture.
Thus one of my little subjects, an intelligent girl of
nine, when asked why she liked a certain landscape,
replied : " Because you see all the flowers and all the
houses and the sea and the little girl with the basket."
Again, a picture of a cavalier is liked " because he's

got on a pretty hat, and pretty curly hair, and earrings, and a lovely black jacket." Here the beauty of individual objects seems to be felt, and this is exactly typical of the child's attitude towards pictures, the apparent absence of any feeling of the *unity* of the pictures being just as striking.

I had a number of different objects painted upon a sheet of paper, such as a large flower, a small bird, a boy with a ship, &c., all scattered about the paper without any connection between the various objects. Yet apparently it was regarded as a picture by the little children of six or seven, to whom I showed it among picture postcards of the same size. Its lack of unity did not seem to strike them as a fault. It was a " nice picture " because " there was a boat," or a " nice flower," or a " little bird " on it. Of course in a test like this one must allow for the fact that very few young children would venture to criticise such a picture shown to them by a comparative stranger. One has to rely chiefly upon more subtle signs to determine whether they realised that this " picture " was quite different from the other pictures.

In another series of experiments pictures were shown to German school children, uneducated adults, educated adults, and finally to an artist. The pictures included two portraits—one of a handsome man but a bad representation, the other of an ugly man well portrayed. The youngest children showed no signs of looking at the pictures from an artistic point of view ; there was no thought of the pictures as representations, no reference to composition, form, or even colour, and no thought of the artist's skill.

Amongst somewhat older children there appear frequently references to colour, occasionally to form, and still more rarely to general impression. Still later come judgments from the artist's point of view, and here again they first have reference to individual details rather than to general effect.

The uneducated adults showed remarkable resemblance to the young children, seldom judging the picture as a whole or as a work of art, points of view which are constantly taken by the more cultured adults. The technique of the pictures naturally attracted the attention especially of the artist.

A comparison of the preferences of the children with those of adults was also made by Professor Mary Calkins. Her subjects were 300 children—from Kindergarten, Primary, and Grammar Schools—and 150 university students, one half being freshmen and one half seniors. Three pictures only were used, and each represented a woman's half-figure. Picture 1 was chiefly notable for its colouring, and depicted the head and shoulders of a girl in Quaker cap and mantle. Picture 2 was notable for beauty of form, being an uncoloured photograph of Chantron's "Souvenir." "The face is slightly turned away, and a high light falls on the beautiful features, on the wistful upturned eyes, on the soft hair knotted in the neck, and on the delicate outlines of the shoulders, arm, and back, from which the garment has fallen away." Picture 3 represented "the buoyant figure of a winged aureoled angel" playing a violin, "with so serious an expression in her wide-opened eyes." The special characteristics of picture 3 are thus its religious associations and suggestions.

The method of the experiment was as follows. Pictures 1 and 2 were shown to the subject, and he was asked which he preferred. The picture selected was then compared with picture 3, and again the subject was asked which he preferred. Taking the first choice, we find that, of the children, about 88 per cent. of each group (Kindergarten, Primary, and Grammar School) preferred the coloured picture 1 to picture 2. Of the freshmen 55 per cent. preferred picture 1, and of the seniors only 38 per cent. preferred picture 1. Many were doubtless affected by details, but the broad result is that, to children, beauty of colour appeals more than does beauty of form and of light and shade without colour, while the reverse is the case with the senior students.

When the second choice was made the coloured picture No. 1 was easily beaten by the religious picture No. 3 among the Kindergarten and Primary School children, picture 3 being preferred in about 76 per cent. of the possible choices. The coloured picture, however, is still the most popular on the second choice with the Grammar School children.

Of the college students about 50 per cent. transfer their allegiance to picture 3, the rest remaining true to their first choice—those who had preferred picture 2 being more faithful to it than were those who had first chosen the coloured picture 1.

An unfortunate flaw in the method of these experiments was the necessity of presenting one and only one of the pictures twice. Thus picture 3 would have the advantage of novelty when compared with the winner of pictures 1 and 2—an advantage which was probably very considerable in the case of many children, though some, on the other hand, may have stuck to their first choice, partly *because* they had already chosen it. The ambiguity of the results might have been avoided by using four cards, the winner of A and B being compared, after an interval, with the winner of C and D.*

A careful analysis was made of the reasons given

---

* Possibly the bare arm and shoulder displayed in picture 2 put it at a disadvantage with the young children, who are proper little conventionalists, and pay great attention to the dress of people in pictures. One of my little subjects objected to the "Virgin Consolatrix" because the mother depicted there with bare arms was "not properly dressed."

for the choices.   A remarkable increase with age was
noticed in the number of negative reasons given—*i.e.*
explanations of preference for one picture based upon
the dislike of the other.   These negative reasons constituted only one-fiftieth of all the reasons given by
the younger children, but one-sixth of those of the
fourteen-year-old children and over one-fifth of those
of the students.   Colour was given as a reason for
preference most frequently by the Grammar School
children, then by the Primary School children, then
by the infants, and least often, proportionately, by
the college students.   References to detail constituted
75 per cent. of the infants' reasons for liking pictures, but only 10 per cent. of those of the Grammar
School children, and only 5 per cent. of the students'
reasons.   References to beauty of form and of expression are rare among the children.   The influence
of religious association is at its highest among the
infants, and then among the other children, scarcely
appearing at all among the students.   Yet the *general*
suggestiveness and meaning of the pictures is obviously of growing influence as age increases, almost
its earliest presence being apparent among the Grammar School children, one of whom, a girl of thirteen,
preferred the picture of the angel, " because you can
think more about it."   The " realness " of the picture
is never mentioned by the youngest children, but is
often mentioned among the Grammar School children
and students, especially among the senior students.

The only marked differences observed between the
sexes was that the girls more often noticed the face
and its expression in the picture.

As a further general result of the experiments it was
stated that, leaving apart the Kindergarten children,
there is no type of choice made by adults which is
not also represented among the children.   Further,
although children seem to be determined by colour, in

making their choice, to a much greater extent than are adults, it by no means follows that a child is sure to prefer a coloured to an uncoloured picture (as has too often been assumed)—a result very emphatically borne out by some as yet incomplete experiments of my own upon Elementary School children.

Experiments with Adults.—We have seen that children rarely seem to enjoy a picture as a work of art. It is true that some of my own subjects, even as young as seven, have said they liked a picture because it was " like a real baby," or sea, or what not. But it is doubtful whether such remarks imply that there is any thought of or pleasure in the idea that it is a good representation. The consciousness of the excellence of a picture merely as a representation, apart from the pleasingness of the things represented, tends to make one speak, occasionally at least, of the excellence of the artist's work, and this rarely occurs in children before the age of twelve or fourteen, unless they have had special training.*

Now it is noticeable that in some adults this point of view is also lacking, or at least it has little influence in determining their appreciation of pictures. The difference of their attitude from that of others was well brought out in some tests I made upon some fifty adults with thirty-six reproductions of pictures, famous and otherwise. We will take, for example, Rembrandt's portrait of himself as an officer. Many find the picture highly pleasing, and speak of the

* I do not wish to imply that the thought of the artist's skill is desirable. From an æsthetic point of view it is doubtless a disturbing element which prevents the observer " losing himself " completely in the picture itself. Yet the thought of such artistic skill hovers close where there is a keen appreciation of the picture *as* a picture and not merely as a suggester of agreeable objects, as it generally is to a young child. Especially in speaking of the picture, after enjoying it, does the thought tend to occur.

excellence of the portraiture as such : " character emanates from every line," " there is a suggestion of strength, the man seems alive," " the artist has put force of character and much expression into the portrait," and so on. Some of these subjects do not like the face of the man as a man, but their appreciation of the excellent way in which he is depicted seems to overcome this. There is a second group of subjects, represented by the following comments : " As a work of art, lovely, but the face does not attract. There are signs of weakness about the mouth, and the eyes look peevish. On the whole, the picture is displeasing." " A masterpiece in portrait-painting, the colouring, &c., being excellent. But it calls up the idea of dark and gloomy times when such men were a terror to the country. The picture is displeasing on the whole."

To a third group of subjects the excellence of the portraiture does not seem to occur. Their judgment is almost entirely determined by their liking, or more often dislike, of the man as represented. " The face looks crueller the longer I look at it "; " pleasing features, such as the dress, are counteracted by the haughty expression "; " the pucker in the brow is irritating, and the features are heavy." This attitude is obviously nearer the naïve realism of the child. The first group represent a more developed artistic attitude. The determination of the point at which such individuals develop beyond the ideal æsthetic attitude and assume one which is too technical or professional must be left to the æsthetician, as must the allied problem as to whether an excellent expression even of the ugly is really always beautiful, as some have asserted.

Another grouping of subjects can be made on the basis of their judgments respecting a picture of a very different type—the " Virgin Consolatrix." In this picture a mother, whose dead child lies prone upon the ground, has flung herself in despair upon the knees of the Virgin. Almost all find this an impressive picture. Some indeed find it overwhelmingly sad, and these are led to dislike the picture. It is noticeable that the only two mothers to whom I showed the picture were of this type. One stated that she used to like this picture well before she had a child of her own, but that now it was too sad. Another group, however, were attracted by the pathos of the picture and the feeling of sympathy it called forth, or they found the sadness, which at first repelled them, more than compensated by the deeper significance of the picture, or by the very excellence and completeness with which sorrow had been portrayed in the picture. In general, it seemed that those whose attention was drawn chiefly to their own feelings, inspired by the picture, found it displeasing. Such are comparable with the subjective type described in the chapter on colour. They included one or two individuals apparently of a fairly high degree of æsthetic culture, but on the average, so far as one could judge, they appeared not to have the keen and developed appreciation of art shown by most of the other group. For these latter the sadness was an element represented in the picture—" read into " the prostrate mother, not felt so much as a distracting feeling of their own. In other words, with them empathy was more prominent than sympathy, though, of course, even the subjective type of person had first to feel that the unhappy mother was suffering, before he could sympathise with her. The least satisfactory individuals from the point of view of æsthetic appreciation would appear to be those who felt *no* sadness in looking at the picture, and for whom it had little depth of meaning. For most of these the picture was " indifferent," and their comments were some-

times confined to the remarks about the colour tone
of the picture or to such side issues as the practices
of the Roman Catholic Church, associated with the
picture of the Virgin.

Very varying effects of a very realistic picture of
a winter day were shown. The picture showed a
village scene, in which a few scattered folk were
fighting against wind and snow in the dusk of twi-
light. Persons of a subjective type remark that it
" has a depressing effect," " gives a feeling almost of
physical discomfort," " seems to strike a chill through
one," " the attitude of the old man makes one want
to draw up the shoulders as though one felt the cold
wind blowing the snow about." To none of these
subjects is the picture pleasing. The suggestion of
discomfort is strong enough to make them feel it
keenly. But in other cases, the excellence of the
representation, even of the bitter cold, is so felt that
the picture is liked. To these the very vividness
of the suggestion of wintry storm with which the
villagers are struggling is a point in favour of the
picture, though they recognise the unpleasantness of
the elements themselves. Then again there are the
strenuous folk to whom the storm appears a glorious
thing in itself. Thus one writes : " The picture is
very pleasing. The sight of the man battling with
the elements is suggestive of cold and wind ; but I
imagine him battling with the elements and having
a sense of internal comfort." Others, again, are
largely influenced by the associations suggested by
the wintry scene. The picture is pleasant because
it suggests skating and snowballing, or because it
recalls " Bleak House." Another of a more imaginative mind sees in the picture a reminder of the
marvels of the physical universe, with its succession
of seasons, and a symbol of man as in some sense a
victim of environment.

CHAPTER VII.

EXPERIMENTS WITH PICTURES (*continued*).

Types of Judgments upon Pictures.—It seems possible to divide most judgments upon pictures into four types similar to those already discussed in the chapter upon colour—viz. objective, subjective, associative, and character or expression.

I will take the opportunity of giving, under these four heads, examples of the enormous variety of reasons given me by adults in the experiments with pictures just mentioned.

The Subjective type, in addition to examples already given, would include judgments partially dependent upon the arousal of such vivid imagery as was mentioned by some of my subjects, thus : " The picture makes me smell the sea and hear the waves." " I can almost feel the cold that makes the poor creatures shrivel up."

Under this heading also would come references to feelings of awe, wonder, sympathy, sadness, and so forth, awakened by the pictures, and adding richness to the æsthetic experience.

It would also comprise cases where the mood of the moment is recognised as the determinant of the judgment ; for example, " Does not appeal to me in my present mood. I only like sad pictures when feeling morbid." Another example of the subjective type is given when a subject feels a definite activity set up by the picture, often a desire to be a sharer in the pleasures or deeds represented. Thus " June in the Austrian Tyrol " makes one subject want to travel—" I should like to be gathering flowers there

6

too." Again, " The mountains make me long to climb them and view the scenery round about," " I like to feel a tossing motion, and the waves in the picture make me long for it."

The Objective type of judgments would include most judgments based upon the clearness or obscurity of the pictures, the colour, light and shade, the variety of objects shown, the grouping and composition of the picture, and the " uncommonness " of a picture, of which one student spoke approvingly. Examples of this kind need scarcely be given.

As we saw in Chapter II., even a simple colour may rouse any of the four perceptive attitudes. So the judgments upon the colour and form, &c., of the pictures may take the form of subjective, associative, or character judgments, though these are less frequent than the objective type.

Examples of the *Associative type* have already been given. They range from the most general type of associations (for example the vague, subconscious memories of happy hours spent among scenes like those depicted in a landscape) to extremely individual cases, having no essential connection with the picture. The most extraordinary example of the latter kind was given by one subject who quite seriously insisted that her judgment of a picture called " Thursday " (depicting monks fishing for Friday's dinner) was affected by the memory of a pleasant event which had happened the previous Thursday, the only connection with the picture being the name of the day.

A fairly frequent association was naturally that of the original of the picture reproduced. Occasionally the contrast with the original was in favour of the reproduction. Sometimes, when the print was judged to be a poor one, the memory of the original may be so strong that the reproduction was said to be more pleasing *because* the original is recalled. Some subjects said they were able to " see " the reproductions as though they were coloured like the originals and to enjoy them as such.

Character (or *Expression*) *type.*—It must be admitted that the character type has to be interpreted in a very broad way if it is to include most of the remaining kinds of judgments, and perhaps Expression would be a better term than Character. Perhaps the closest parallels to the character judgments upon colours are afforded by those subjects who read something like human feeling into pictures of nature, for example in these comments : " The big waves swelling impotently, striving for something and never attaining it," " the nodding flowers give a merry note as contrasted with the sombre majesty of the hills."

Next in order would come those cases in which character or feeling is read into the animals depicted. Thus one appreciation of a country scene includes the suggestion that the dog is " feeling proud of his responsibility " of looking after the cattle while his master is talking with a friend. Several subjects, too, enter vividly into the feelings of a dog represented as about to share his poor master's meal. Very few animals appeared in the pictures used, so examples of this kind are rare.

Such remarks both about nature and animals show that empathy is present : subjects feel into things experiences resembling in some way those they have had themselves. It is obvious that this will occur much more naturally with the representations of human beings. This is indeed essential for the full enjoyment of most figure pictures. It is thus we enter into the meaning of such pictures. Judgments based upon expression are of this type, whether the expression of character or of feeling in the individual depicted, or expression of meaning or of an emotional situation as given by a group of persons.

[Of course such perceptions of character and feeling are dependent upon association in the sense that all our mental development is so in part. Memories of many past experiences teach us to recognise and interpret more exactly the signs of feeling and of character in another person. Some signs of emotion indeed are understood and responded to appropriately by an infant whose own experience is far too limited to explain such response. Some comprehension, then, of outward expressions of some of the emotions seems to be congenital. Where, however, association does enter into our interpretation of the expression of emotion and character in pictures, the reader will readily distinguish in a broad way the general and essential nature of its work, from the part that associations play in such judgments as we have called Associative. Yet it must be admitted that it is impossible to draw a hard and fast line between the two.]

Closely connected with the preceding is the judgment of a picture according to the *idea* it expresses, or the degree of perfection with which it expresses that idea. There is " character " in many pictures, at least in a derivative sense of the word, for the artist has written there the symbol of his thought. But if this is to be understood and appreciated, there must be responsive character in the one who sees the picture, to enable him to read again into those symbols the meaning they are meant to convey.

There is a further and very important aspect of a picture which is of great influence in determining its æsthetic value—namely, its unity. This is of course partly a question of colour combination and partly, as we have seen, of balance and symmetry. But the highest unity involves also unity of meaning and purpose, possible, indeed often more evident, in the presence of contrast. It may not be too fanciful to class even this aspect of a picture as one of its character-aspects. For the character of a person is essentially the unity of the various aspects of his nature. One who lacks such unity, who is the sport of every varying impulse and isolated desire, we regard as essentially lacking in character.

This necessity of unity in a picture is based upon the psychological law of attention to which we have referred in both the preceding chapters. If there is to be full æsthetic enjoyment in the contemplation of a picture, attention must not be frustrated by having entirely disconnected items thrust before it.

Let the reader ask another person to take a momentary glance at the following row of letters (not exposing them long enough for the subject to read the letters off individually) and then ask him to write down what he saw—R H E T R C A A C. Then let him show the letters arranged to form the principal word in the heading of this section (p. 83), and he will find their instantaneous apprehension enormously facilitated. It has indeed been found that several groups of letters, united to form half a dozen words connected in meaning, can be apprehended in a fraction of a second with the same ease as half a dozen letters which do not form a unity. Now in a complex object like a picture, interconnection of elements makes not only rapid apprehension easier, but facilitates continuous attention. Many details may be allowed in a picture, and their variety may make it all the more interesting, but they must be bound into a unity with *meaning* connecting them if our desire to take in the picture as a whole is not to be thwarted.

We have not room to discuss more fully the interesting variety of judgments given in these experiments with pictures, as, for example, the influence of the knowledge of the artist's name and his reputation, or the frequent references to the *usual* effects of such and such pictures, as *e.g.* " I always like pictures of the sea," and " I don't like pictures of people eating."

Doubtless it would not be possible to classify some of the judgments given under any of the four heads we have used. But the distinction of the four types is broadly clear, and furthermore, many individuals seem to make so much more use of a certain type of judgment—given an adequate variety of good pictures —that they may be said to belong to that type, and this may give us some clue as to the degree of æsthetic development which they have attained.

Judging from the impressions obtained by reading the appreciations of very many of the subjects, it is clear that a fair proportion of judgments of the character or expression type are sure to be made by subjects who have a really keen appreciation of pictorial art.

Associations may occur with all persons at all stages of æsthetic culture, but a frequent use of them as the main basis of the appreciation of a picture (as, for example, " I like it because it reminds me of my native town," or " because it suggests a sail on the Clyde which I enjoyed very much ") seems to be indicative of a low degree of æsthetic development, at least in this department of art.

We have already seen that the subjective attitude may be disturbing to the enjoyment of pictures, particularly sad pictures. But it is sometimes hard to say whether the subjective attitude is not one which really only *follows* the moments of real appreciation of the picture, when the subject tries to describe his attitude and the reasons for his liking or disliking. This, I think, was the case with several subjects whom I knew personally to have a keen appreciation of art, and who gave several subjective judgments.

The records indicate that a few of the subjects had very little interest in pictures, some confessing that this was so and that they were bored by pictures. Now the judgments of these were almost entirely objective or associative, such as comments upon the colour, its suitability or unsuitability, the resemblance to reality, the clearness or obscurity of the picture, and so forth. Of course there are occasions when such comments are the natural and indeed the most suitable ones. But apparently individuals who confine themselves largely to this type of judgments seem to have little real appreciation of the beauty of pictures.

It is notable that such objective (and to a less extent associative and subjective) judgments are just the kind of reasons given by the youngest children tested in our experiments, when they do not content themselves with references to the objects in the picture. Character judgments are a comparatively late development.

I may conclude this section by giving as fairly typical the number of the various kinds of judgments given by a subject who has a keen appreciation of pictorial art, but without special training except that given by visits to picture galleries.

Objective judgments	6
Subjective judgments	6
Associative judgments	6
Character judgments	9
Unclassified judgments	2

The Effect of Short Time Exposures of Pictures.— Dr. E. von Ritook recently carried out a thorough investigation of the effects produced by exposing pictures for only 2, 5, 7 or 10 seconds. Nine subjects were tested and 130 pictures were used, including photographs of architecture and statuary, some of the pictures being coloured. The pictures were thrown upon a screen in a dark room by means of a powerful lantern, the subject being warned just before the picture was exposed. He then gave as full an account as possible of his experience, which was carefully recorded. It was hoped by this method to get a sort of cross-section of the æsthetic experience, and to isolate elements which would mingle in the course of a longer exposure. Of course, with such a short exposure, especially when only 2 seconds was given, sometimes the picture was not completely apprehended or understood, and sometimes the colour was not noticed. Yet it was found that even then the picture might be pleasing, merely as an arrangement of light and shade, a primitive form of æsthetic experience that no doubt retains some influence even in the full enjoyment of a picture.

A curious illusion of reality was sometimes experienced as the result of these short exposures. Portraits were sometimes felt to be real people, and to one man the portrait of a woman appeared so like reality that it caused a feeling of bashfulness. Another illusion was the imagining that the picture was coloured when it was not. Empathy, of which we have already spoken, occurred even in some of the shortest exposures, though not so frequently as in the longer ones. Two subjects (said to be of a "motor" type) showed a strong tendency to imitate movements represented in the pictures : thus one says she tends to hold herself like the virgin in the picture in order to comprehend her feeling more clearly. With these two subjects imitative movement seems to initiate empathy, but it does not seem by any means essential to it ; indeed imitation sometimes proved a hindrance to the full enjoyment of a picture. Possibly such imitation belongs to a primitive stage which passes away with most people.

Children sometimes imitate actions which are referred to while stories are being read to them, apparently to make the realisation more vivid, but this tendency does not seem nearly so common with adults.

To some subjects the space represented in the picture seemed very real. They felt themselves as it were *in* that space. Thus one speaks of finding himself in the dwelling and being disturbed by the presence of a nun represented in the picture, as he wished to be alone. Some felt the pleasure of the wide open space around them, as though they were themselves placed in the landscape.

Perhaps one of the most interesting results of this investigation was the fact that pictures were found pleasing so often even with the short exposure of two seconds. The number of " pleasing " judgments did not greatly increase with the increasing length of the exposure. Yet the full significance of the picture could not always be realised in so short a time. This would tend to be more prominent with longer exposures, and would occupy the attention more than would that immediate impression, which becomes prominent in a rapid exposure. Consequently we probably tend to speak less of that immediate first impression in giving our reasons for liking or disliking a picture, yet doubtless its influence remains and forms a not unimportant element in the total effect produced by the picture.

The Effect of repeatedly seeing a Picture forms an interesting problem in view of the fact that we are frequently looking at the same pictures in our own houses. Fifty pictures were shown to subjects in turn, the judgment on each being recorded. This was repeated with the same pictures for five days. On the sixth day the pictures were again shown to the subjects, but now they were exposed for five minutes, and the subjects were asked for their judgments at the end of that time as well as at the beginning. The pictures were also shown again one month and also three months later. Then the whole series of experiments was repeated with fifty new pictures—a good example of the thoroughness of the work of this investigator, Professor L. J. Martin. With two out of the five subjects the pictures were liked distinctly more on the occasion of their second exposure than they had been on the first, thus supporting the statement that " without previous practice many fine and high æsthetic impressions escape one." The five minutes' exposure, again, generally resulted in still more favourable judgments; and taking the results as a whole, one can certainly conclude that such a repetition of the exposure of pictures, if these are sufficiently good, tends to make them more rather than less pleasing. With many pictures the result would doubtless be the reverse. But naturally the more there is in a picture the more will familiarity with it improve it for us.

The Effect of looking at a Picture continuously.—Professor Martin was able to persuade three subjects to look at seven pictures for forty-five minutes each. It may appear surprising that the subjects could keep their attention fixed upon a picture for such a length of time, but they seem to have done so, with occasional aberrations. The results show, as we should expect, that as a rule the pleasure derived from looking at a picture continuously rises to a certain maximum and then decreases. But it is notable that only very occasionally does a pleasing picture become actually displeasing even with so long an exposure as three quarters of an hour. And very rarely does a picture originally displeasing become positively pleasing, though it frequently becomes more endurable.

It was noted by all the subjects that with the prolonging of the exposure all movement in the picture seemed to cease, and that the picture seemed to grow flat—*i.e.*, lose its perspective. Thus one subject says, after a picture has been exposed thirty-five minutes, " The water seems a white streak unless I wonder if it will still flow ; then it does." Another says of a woman in a cottage interior, " The figure seems to have stopped work to pose," and of Hals's " The Jolly Man," " The man smiled at first ; then the smile ceased and the mouth just seemed open." The mother in Raphael's " La Belle Jardinière " " seemed as if she were going to do something at first ; then she did not, and I was tired of watching."

Very definite " sensations " (more strictly vivid images) seem to have been experienced by the subjects in looking at these pictures. Thus during the exposure of Rubens' " Descent from the Cross " one subject " could feel the pulling on the teeth of the cloth held in the mouth of one of the men, and the muscular strength he was obliged to exert." In looking at this picture all the subjects " felt " in some sense the physical pain in connection with the taking down of Christ's body. One subject (a woman) was especially delighted with pictures in which a child was represented as held in its mother's arms, and spoke repeatedly of " delightful physical sensations arising from the sense of touch in connection with the child's flesh, which she experiences on the seeing of such a picture." Professor Martin does not say at what period of the prolonged exposure such vivid imagery occurs most frequently, but we have already seen that it may occur even with quite short exposures.

Illusions in looking at Pictures.—Some of my own subjects stated that they could at will see black and white reproductions of pictures as coloured, but this apparently meant that they could imagine the colours so vividly that the black and white reproduction of the picture became practically the equivalent of a coloured picture for them—so far as æsthetic enjoyment was concerned. We saw, however, that in the case of the very short exposures of pictures given by Miss Von Ritook, some subjects actually thought the pictures were coloured. A still more striking case was discovered by Professor Martin. One of her subjects, who drew and painted in watercolours, frequently spoke of seeing colour in the black and white reproductions, although she *knew* that they were only black and white ; and when asked to copy two of the pictures she actually reproduced them in colours, affirming that this represented exactly what she saw. She expressed great surprise that the experimenter never saw such colours. One other subject was found who similarly saw colours in black and white pictures. Purple was the colour most often seen, and it was seen especially in the deep shadows. The most striking thing is that when a series of one hundred pictures were described by her, as she saw them, and coloured sketches of them taken, and then the same process gone through a month later, in the vast majority of cases the colours seen were the same or almost exactly the same on the second occasion as they had been a month previously, though the record had not been referred to in the meantime.

Such illusions of colour occurred more readily with large pictures than with small, and it was found that they were greatly influenced by what the subject had been doing during the previous hour or so. Thus if she had spent the preceding time in examining Japanese prints, the pictures looked at during the experiments following would tend to appear like Japanese prints. The kind of weather and the health and mood of the subject also had their effect, the colours being seen more vividly on bright sunny days and when the subject was unusually well and cheerful.

It is noteworthy that this subject had exceedingly vivid visual imagery, and that when asked to recall a colour, purple was often imagined first. Now it appears that in earlier years she had had considerable training of an impressionist kind in painting. Particularly had she been told to " see purple," and in response she called up the colour through an act of memory and superimposed it upon what was under examination. Thus the imagining of a colour, especially purple, became a habit not requiring an effort of will.

Another of Professor Martin's subjects had illusions of a different kind. She imagined she saw, not colours, but additional objects in the picture. Out of 1170 exposures of pictures there were 374 cases of illusions of this kind. Very frequently these took the form of the addition of something to the vague background : *e.g.* in Rosa Bonheur's " Sheep in a Meadow," a sloping hill was seen dotted with sheep. Sometimes a face or figure was reduplicated, or a figure partly seen was completed. Seven times there was a permanent sense of some unseen presence in the background. The method followed in this last experiment was as follows. The subject looked at the picture long enough to be able to recognise it again, and then turned it over and recorded her impressions. It seems possible and even probable that many of the illusions were really illusions of memory. But there are sufficient indications in the record to show that they were not all of that nature, and that the additional objects were not only vividly imagined, but actually located in the picture. It is notable that illusions occurred by far the most frequently with the pictures that were best liked. It would

seem that pleasurable stimulation was favourable to
such active imagery, as indeed it is to other kinds of
imagination. In their turn the illusions may have
added to the æsthetic value of the pictures in which
they occurred.

It is a striking fact that among such a small group
of subjects there should be found three who had such
decided illusions of colour or of content as we have
just described. Possibly they are much more common
than most people suspect.

The Pairing of Pictures.—The question as to
whether two pictures will " pair well " or " go together " is to some people one of considerable practical interest. It will be readily agreed that a desire
for very close resemblance of two pictures to form a
pair is a sign of undeveloped æsthetic taste, as is the
love of exact geometrical symmetry between the two
sides of a picture. A very different type is found in
those persons who have no desire to see neighbouring
pictures on a wall resemble one another in any way,
and who disapprove of attempts to pair pictures.
However, thinking it would be interesting to discover
the basic principles of such pairing when it is done,
I took the same thirty-six pictures used in the experiments described on p. 78, and grouped the cards
into pairs, some good pairs, as it seemed to me, and
some bad. I presented these cards in pairs to some
thirty subjects, and asked them to say whether they
liked them *as pairs.* They were also asked to say
whether their liking for either card was affected by
the presence of the other card.

In the first place, one or two subjects, and those
among the most intelligent and the keenest lovers of
pictures, found some difficulty in apprehending the
cards together in any sense. Each picture retained
to the full its own individuality, they said, and would
not be " paired " with the other.

To the majority, however, such apprehension of two pictures as a pair presented no difficulty, and it proved that the pairing might have a very great and very varying influence upon the individual pictures. If we indicate the two pictures by A and B, then if A and B were each pleasing when taken alone, they might be displeasing as a pair, or each of them might be improved by pairing with the other. If A and B were each of them displeasing when taken alone, nevertheless the pair A B might be agreeable, owing to their mutual support. (Of course the pictures might "pair well" and yet still be displeasing as a pair, because of the unpleasantness of each individual picture.) If A were very pleasing and B displeasing, the pairing may result in the improvement of B, giving a pleasing pair, or in the spoiling of A, resulting in a displeasing pair. As one subject put it, B "led one to look for something," and this was supplied by A, so that the unsatisfactory card B was saved by its neighbour and the pair made pleasing as a whole.

The various reasons given for two pictures pairing well (or badly) may be roughly divided into two main groups : (1) those having reference to *similarity*, and (2) those having reference to *contrast*. Further, these may be (*a*) similarity (or contrast) of form, colour, composition, &c. ; (*b*) similarity (or contrast) of meaning ; or (*c*) similarity (or contrast) of feelings produced by the respective pictures.

The same subject who, in the experiments with single pictures previously described, gave chiefly objective reasons for liking or disliking the pictures, and who confessed to having little or no interest in pictures, now in the pairing experiments based her judgments again chiefly upon form, colour arrangement, &c. She was also persistent in her demand for similarity. In general it appears from the records that those

who care for pictures most and understand them
best are most alive to the possibility of contrast (at
least to contrast of meaning and feeling) as a basis
for the pairing of pictures. Yet of course all real
contrast implies some similarity, and the change
from one picture to another must not be without its
connecting link. Here, again, great individual differences occur. Thus two subjects, both keen lovers
of pictures, were asked to select the best picture
among eight to pair with " The Goose Girl " (Prinsep).
One of the pictures, a sunset over the sea, was completely ruled out by subject A, as being impossible
to pair with " The Goose Girl," owing to the absence
of human life and interest (except two small fishing-
boats) in the sunset scene. Subject B, however,
selected this very picture as the best picture of all
the eight to pair with " The Goose Girl." For to
him the dominant note of " The Goose Girl," the
thoughtful expression of the central figure, had in it
something of mystery, and the mood aroused in the
observer found its best outlet in the lonely and
mystical beauty of the sunset scene.

The hindering effect of too great a contrast of
meaning was frequently felt when one picture represented some historical scene while the other was
purely imaginative. The mental jerk was felt from
the attitude of mind in which our knowledge of facts
determines largely our apprehension of a picture, to
the attitude in which the imagination is left almost
entirely free. " Historic associations crowd in with
picture A," wrote one subject, " but they are useless
with picture B." Other subjects disliked the pairing of a picture representing an event recorded in
the Old Testament (" The Parting of Ruth and
Naomi ") with one representing a mythological event
(" The Return of Persephone "). Even though a
strong connection was perceived in the bond of affec-

tion between the women, in the one case parting and in the other reuniting, yet the " groups of ideas " to which these stories belonged were felt to be too divergent for the two pictures to be thought of and liked as a pair. Here again, then, we meet with that psychological principle to which we have had to refer several times before, that of *facilitation of attention*. If the æsthetic experience is to be enjoyed to the full, there must be no rude interruption in the course of the mental apprehension of the object. Adequate change to maintain interest and to stimulate intellectual activity to a certain degree there must be.   But as in a curved line there must be no sudden change entirely inconsistent with what the line as a whole pretends to be, and as in a picture there must be no element which has no connection with the picture as a whole, so, if we are seeking to pair two pictures, there must not be too great a change from one to the other, suddenly confronting us with the necessity of changing our whole mental attitude.

That is the negative side of the principle. Stated positively it is that in the apprehension of a beautiful curve one part of it gives us a clue to the nature of the rest ; in a good picture " everything helps everything else " ; and in the case of a good pair of pictures the meaning of the one, the feeling or mood which it creates in us, puts us into an attitude which is especially favourable for the full appreciation of the partner picture—a preparation which is sometimes so effective, as we have seen, as to turn a picture actually displeasing in itself into an added source of enjoyment when conjoined with another.

CHAPTER VIII.

EXPERIMENTS WITH MUSICAL INTERVALS.

The Types in Musical Experiments.—As we have
seen, different people may take very different attitudes
towards a colour or a picture, resulting in judgments
of varying kinds, subjective, associative, &c. In
order to discover whether similar attitudes are
adopted towards musical chords, I performed a series
of experiments with musical intervals played on the
piano. The octave, the major and minor thirds and
sixths, and the other intervals within the octave
were played one at a time to a group of people.*
They were provided with paper on which they were
asked to record the judgments about the chords
played, stating whether they found them very pleasing, pleasing, slightly pleasing, indifferent, slightly
displeasing, &c., adding if possible the reason why.
Each interval was played twice with a brief pause
between, the notes being held down for three seconds
on each occasion. Over 150 persons were thus tested.

The answers showed to a remarkable extent attitudes similar to those assumed towards colours, about
half the persons tested adopting a certain attitude
so frequently that they might reasonably be classed
as belonging to the subjective, the objective, character
or associative type.

The aspect of the intervals which appealed to subjects of the *objective type* is shown by the following
comments : perfect blending, full and round, one note

---

* Here and elsewhere the term interval is used to refer to
two notes played *simultaneously*. The term " bichord " may
be used for the same purpose.

competes with the other for prominence, the notes are too wide apart, and so on.

The *subjective type* thought especially of the influence of the notes upon *themselves*—thus : jars on the nerves, gives a creepy feeling, makes one draw a deep breath, feeling of lethargy produced, causes melancholy, stirring, makes me think my cares are over for a time.

The *associative type* gave most frequently as their reasons for liking an interval the fact that it recalled either some source of a similar sound (church bells, gong, &c.) or some piece of music.

The *character type*, as in experiments with colour, read something of personality into the notes. They were described as follows : decided, assertive, meek, sullen, happy, lacking joviality, hopeful, bold, and forceful. People of this type seemed to get more enjoyment out of the harmonious intervals than did those of the other types. Indeed the assumption of this mental attitude sometimes resulted in a discord being pleasing.

Fourteen of the subjects tested by Mr. Bullough with colours were also tested by Dr. C. S. Myers with musical tones and intervals, and all except two persons proved to be of the same type in their attitudes towards colours and musical notes. Dr. Myers concludes that these individual differences in mental attitudes are of " enormous importance in determining opinion as to what is of fundamental æsthetic importance in music." *

Æsthetic Value of the Attitudes in Music.— Before considering the æsthetic values of these various kinds of attitudes we must distinguish between two kinds of associations in the judgments on musical inter-

* For a much more detailed analysis of the types, the reader is referred to the experiments by Dr. C. S. Myers. See bibliography to chaps. viii. and ix.

vals. One kind we may call *musical associations*. The
subjects frequently found that they could not hear and
judge a musical interval by itself. The suggestion of
a following and completing interval was intimately
bound up with it and intensified the pleasure due to
the given interval, or actually made pleasing an interval which quite alone would have been displeasing.
In other words, these musical associations were often
so intimately fused with the impression of the chord
itself as to be inseparable from it. They are frequent with very musical people, and are evidently of
far higher value in the æsthetic scale than are such
associations as the following, which occur frequently
in the judgments of musically untrained Elementary
School children—" reminds me of a church bell,"
" of a syren," " of a tin can being squashed."
These latter may be called *non-musical* or *non-fused*
associations.

In order to get some evidence as to the æsthetic
value of the various attitudes, I calculated the frequency with which each type of attitude was accompanied by the judgment " very pleasing." This
seems a fair method, for even if there may be æsthetic
value without any pleasure (which is doubtful), it is
still probable that, when judgments are given on a
series of simple objects such as colours or musical
chords, the most pleasing will usually be found the
most æsthetic. Hence there will be a close resemblance between the order of the degree of pleasingness of the experiences produced by such colours or
chords, and the order of the æsthetic value of these
experiences. Accordingly, in the following table the
various aspects have been arranged according to the
frequency with which each type of judgment was
accompanied by the further judgment " very pleasing." Parallel to this is given Mr. E. Bullough's
estimate of the order of the æsthetic value of the

aspects in the case of colours. Mr. Bullough's criterion, however, is a different one from mine—viz. the extent to which the attention is concentrated upon the object itself, rather than upon non-fused associations or on the self.

TABLE SHOWING ORDER OF ÆSTHETIC VALUE OF TYPES OF JUDGMENT.

IN EXPERIMENTS ON MUSICAL INTERVALS.	IN MR. E. BULLOUGH'S EXPERIMENTS ON COLOURS.
I. Character.	I. Character.
II. Musical (fused) associations.	II. Fused associations.
III. Objective.	III. Objective.
IV. Subjective.	IV. Non-fused associations.
V. Associations other than musical (non-fused).	V. Subjective (or physiological).

It will be seen that there is a remarkable similarity between these two orders.

In experiments with pictures (and as I have also found with poems) it seems possible to form a fairly good estimate of the æsthetic development of an individual according to the extent to which he uses the higher or lower types of these judgments, and it seems likely that the same might be done in music. A full investigation with musical compositions is needed. In some preliminary experiments of my own with selections from Beethoven, Schubert, and Mendelssohn, played on the piano, the types again appear, and there is a suggestion that the dominant type of attitude shown towards the bichords also appears when the same individual expresses a judgment on the renderings of musical compositions.

Sex Differences in Musical Experiments.—In

general I have found women students much more thorough and facile than men in introspective work in other departments of æsthetics, for example with colours. Yet in these music tests fifteen women and only five men had to be classed as of neutral type, because of the poverty of their introspective remarks; and even among these the men average 1·2 character judgments and the women only 0·3. My general impression in reading over the introspective remarks of these 146 subjects was that there were more men than women who were deeply sensitive to the impressions of musical intervals.

This idea is supported by the proportion of judgments of high æsthetic judgment value among the answers of the men and women respectively. The subjects of the experiments included eighty-four women and fifty-two men. If we increase the number of judgments given by the men proportionately, for the sake of ready comparison with those of the women, we find that as regards the highest type of judgment (character) the men surpass the women by 70 per cent., whereas the women give 70 per cent. more of the lowest type of judgment than do the men. It is possible, however, that this apparent sex difference is partly due to a racial difference. For the sixty-two men included thirty-one English and Welsh men, and these gave considerably more judgments of the highest type and fewer of the lowest than did the other men, who were Scots. Yet the Scotsmen taken alone were evidently superior to their fellow countrywomen. On the whole, the investigation certainly suggests that, as colours seem to interest women more than men, musical chords appeal more strongly to men. The fact that women concern themselves more than men with music (for example, as regards the taking of lessons in the playing of the piano) is perhaps a matter of convention, and is not due to any greater sensitivity to music, at least so far as individual tones are concerned.

The Relation between the Consonance and the Pleasingness of Musical Intervals.—Another purpose of the experiments just described was to discover what were the most pleasing musical intervals, and especially to test the assumption sometimes made that the most consonant intervals are the most pleasing.

The following values were assigned for various kinds of judgments on the intervals. Very pleasing 2, pleasing 1, slightly pleasing $\frac{1}{2}$, indifferent 0, slightly displeasing $-\frac{1}{2}$, displeasing -1, very displeasing -2. Adding up the scores of the different intervals we get the following totals :—

TABLE SHOWING ORDER OF POPULARITY OF
THE INTERVALS WITHIN THE OCTAVE.

Major third	324	Tritone	153
Minor third	261	Fifth	139$\frac{1}{2}$
Octave	246$\frac{1}{2}$	Major second	-99
Major sixth	243	Minor seventh	-162
Minor sixth	214	Major seventh	-316
Fourth	157$\frac{1}{2}$	Minor second	-368

As will be seen, this order is very different from the order of degree of consonance.* The major third scores much more than the octave, both the thirds and both the sixths score higher than the more consonant fourth and fifth, and even the tritone (augmented fourth), which has been reckoned on the border line between consonants and dissonants, is found more pleasing on the average than the fifth, the most consonant of all the intervals except the octave.

* For the proper use of the term " consonance," see C. S. Myers's *Experimental Psychology*, 2nd edit., chap. iv., especially pp. 45, 46.

The degree of consonance then is by no means the sole determinant of the pleasingness of an interval, though, of course, taken as a whole the eight consonant intervals are much more pleasing than the four discords.

A curious result which emerged in the course of the experiments was this, that the major third and major sixth was described as sad twice as often as the minor third and minor sixth. Even when a third note is added in these experiments, and the chords *ceg* and *ce♭g* are played, the major chord is still termed sad even more frequently than the minor, though, judging from his own introspection, the present writer is greatly surprised at this result. Thus among about forty adults to whom these chords were played (among twenty other chords), eight persons described the major chord and six persons the minor chord as sad.

This supports the view that the usual effects of the minor key for modern European ears are not due to any natural effect of the minor intervals taken alone. We may suppose that the custom of setting sad songs to minor keys originated without any felt suitability of the key to the ideas, but that gradually, by repetition of the association, we have come to connect the two, so that a piece of music in a minor key now usually appears to us sad or plaintive. In favour of this view, that there is nothing *inherently* sad about the minor key, we have the fact that even in some civilised countries the major key is frequently used for sad songs and the minor sometimes for quite cheerful or even merry ones. Thus we find dance music, and even comic songs, set to a minor key. Further, it is asserted that the music in the minor key played by some primitive peoples, while sounding sad and dirge-like to us, does not appear to be so to the natives. It is noteworthy that five times in the experiments the major third was actually described as "minor" while the minor was never called "minor." Probably this particular major interval was felt to be sad, and was termed minor because of the familiar association of the two in music.

The Development in Young Children of Discrimination between Concords and Discords.—Similar experiments to the above were performed on some 200 Elementary School children between the ages of six and fourteen, taken in small groups. In these experiments I had the assistance of some Training College students. Each student took charge of a child and wrote down what he said about an interval when I played it on the piano. The children were simply asked to say whether they liked the notes or not. For the essential precautions which were taken in these experiments (*e.g.* to guard against suggestion) I must refer the reader to a detailed account elsewhere.* I may state here the main results.

(1) No appreciable preference for concords before discords is discernible before the (average) age of nine, but at this age a very marked advance takes place. The change at this age is most significant, in view of the fact that another investigator found that great advance had taken place by the age of nine in the power of discriminating tone varying in pitch. The average child, he found, improves in this respect more than twice as fast from six to nine years of age as he does in the years from nine to nineteen.

(2) It is not till we reach the age of eleven that we find that the discords show a negative score—*i.e.* are on the average more displeasing than pleasing to the children.

(3) At twelve and thirteen (children of which ages

* See article by the author on the " Æsthetic Appreciation of Musical Intervals among School Children and Adults," *British Journal of Psychology*, vol. vi. p. 200.

were grouped together) we suddenly find changes
which result in an order of preference for the various
intervals which is almost exactly the same as that
given by adults.   It is then only at the age of twelve
or thirteen that (on the average) Elementary School
children, with their musical training almost confined
to school singing, have reached the normal final stage
of development in respect to this essential element
for musical appreciation.

Very different results were obtained in a Preparatory Girls' School, in which nearly every girl over seven
learned some musical instrument, and all of whom
heard good music fairly often.   Here even the little
ones of six and seven show a definite dislike of discords; and by the age of about nine these children
give an order of preference for the various intervals
almost identical with that given by adults, a stage
reached by the Elementary School children only at
the age of twelve.   There is little doubt that this
difference was largely due to the early training of
the Preparatory School girls, and one would be dis-
posed to attribute it entirely to this cause but for
the following evidence of a heredity difference in a
certain capacity necessary for music, between children of the two classes represented by the Elementary
and Preparatory Schools.   Mr. Cyril Burt tested boys
from a Preparatory School and boys from an Elementary School at Oxford in the discrimination of
sounds differing in pitch.*   It was found that the
Preparatory School boys were much more acute in
the discrimination of pitch.   But in this case it
happened that they had not had nearly as much
training in music as the Elementary School boys,
half of whom were choristers and many of whom
learned some musical instrument; while five out of

* See " Experimental Tests of General Intelligence," *British
Journal of Psychology*, vol. iii. p. 125.

thirteen of the Preparatory School boys neither sang nor learned music, and had to be told the meaning of the terms "higher" and "lower" as applied to musical notes.

More numerous tests are needed to make it certain that this difference of the power of discrimination of pitch is a heredity class distinction. If so, it is very difficult to explain. But in any case the part played by discrimination of pitch in determining the appreciation of discords and concords—a more complex process—is unknown; it does not seem to be very important, for the Elementary School children did finally—though at a later age—reach a stage in the discrimination of concords and discords similar to that reached by the Preparatory School children. There can be little doubt that this essential element in the appreciation of music could be developed much earlier than is the case with the majority of children by better training; and if this is the case with the relatively simple discrimination of concords and discords, it is still more likely that training could do much more in reference to the appreciation of music in its fullest sense, with all its complexities of tone, harmony, and rhythm.

The Method of Comparison in Experiments in Æsthetics.—With five subjects I performed a more prolonged series of experiments similar to those just described. In addition to judging single intervals, they were asked to *compare* two intervals one played after the other, and to say which they liked best. One of the objects of these experiments was to discover the value of this method of comparison as a means of investigating problems in æsthetics. I may say that the evidence pointed to its being distinctly inferior to the method of presenting the musical chords one at a time for appreciation and judgment. The very act of comparing is a process which seems

inimical to the æsthetic attitude proper. It leads
to a too purely intellectual attitude, and at least in
experiments with musical chords or with colours this
method of comparison does not seem satisfactory.
With more complex objects such as pictures, for
which the subject may be given his own time and
which have sufficient individuality and power to
make a very decided and permanent impression, the
method may not suffer so much from these defects.
Yet even here a subject must be very careful to let
each picture have its full play upon him, and must
not pass too hurriedly from one to the other. And
further, the very strength of the impression of picture 1 of a pair determines all the more decidedly the
attitude in which he will receive picture 2 which has
to be compared with it ; so much so that, as we saw,
a picture A, which taken alone is found displeasing,
may be liked when judged after picture B, or if found
pleasing when seen alone may be disliked when seen
after picture B.

**The Effect of Repetition and Familiarity in
Music.**—The most remarkable result of the prolonged
experiment with five persons, just mentioned, was
that the discords became much less displeasing to
two of these persons as the experiment proceeded,
rising indeed practically to the level of concords in
pleasingness. It must be noted that this was a very
long series of experiments. Each of the twelve intervals was judged thirty-four times by each subject,
twelve times taken by itself and twenty-two times in
comparison with some other interval. The graph on
page 109 shows the changes in the judgments (very
pleasing, pleasing, slightly pleasing, &c.) on the concords and discords as given by one subject in the
twelve sittings in the experiments in which the intervals were judged alone.

Thus at number 1 sitting the *average* score of the

eight concords was about 1½, *i.e.* between "pleasing" and "very pleasing." The average score of the four discords was about —¾, *i.e.* between "slightly displeasing" and "displeasing." Yet by the end of the experiments the discords were found practically as pleasing as the concords. In the case of another subject the discords were actually found, near the end of the experiments, more pleasing on the average than the concords.

GRAPH INDICATING CHANGE IN THE APPRECIATION OF DISCORDS WITH PRACTICE.

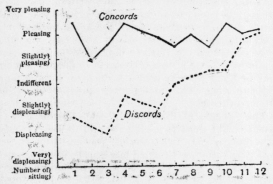

If we turn to the introspective remarks of these subjects we get some clue as to the reason for this remarkable change. It is apparently partly due to a change in æsthetic attitude. Thus one subject at first wrote thus of three of the discords : "unpleasant sensations in the head," "unable to apprehend the notes as one ; they fight," "the start jars." At the end of the experiments he said of the same discords, "interesting, seems to involve mental activity," "plaintive," and "stimulating." The evidence, however, on the whole suggests that there was something more than a mere change of attitude towards the same impression. It suggests that the discords came actually to appear different things ; they were often indeed felt as consonant. One subject, while quite ignorant of his change of attitude towards the discords, thought that they were not being played as often as the concords. Sometimes also the discordance of an interval seemed to disappear when it was replayed after the interval of three seconds.

These results indicate that, even in a series of experiments, if sufficiently long, some adaptation to discords may take place similar to that which has taken place within the history of European music. There we find progress marked by the admission of intervals previously forbidden. Chords which at one time were regarded as ugly discords have come to be used freely in modern music. Even the major third, now the most popular interval, judging from our previous experiments, was inadmissible at one period. These changes, which have appeared and been accepted in the history of music, seem to be of a permanent nature. They may be caused and fixed by the accustoming of children to the music of their generation at the period of special plasticity for such adaptation. Unfortunately, I did not discover the curious adaption to discords in my experiments until my subjects were scattered. Otherwise I should like to have found whether there was any connection between the adaptability to discords and a liking for some modern composers. I may say, however, that one of the two subjects who showed this adaptation to discords finds delight in the most characteristic and extreme " harmonies " of modern composers ; while the only other subject, among the five, who showed this adaptation to a marked degree, though not acquainted with the most modern music, declared that Wagner was her favourite composer.

It is possible that the kind of adaptation which appeared in these experiments may have been similar to that which Max Meyer found in some experiments with quarter tone music, made on the model of some Asiatic tunes. Most of his subjects found this music at first highly disagreeable, but it became pleasing to some after a dozen or more repetitions. He himself found the music at first very unpleasant, but later it became more and more beautiful. On the other hand some of his subjects maintained their dislike of the music almost unchanged throughout the experiments. Meyer thinks that they had already acquired such a definite set in their way of thinking musically that they were very slow to adapt themselves to such novel music. These may resemble those of my own subjects who maintained their dislike of the discords. And this difference may be one of the causes of the difference between those who can appreciate more modern harmonies and those who find them intolerable.

If such very striking changes can take place in the appreciation of discords in a series of experiments, who can say what combinations of notes may not be enjoyed in the music of the future, as the successive modernists of each generation accustom their hearers to newer harmonies, and especially when they are heard frequently by the more plastic ears of youth? It is, however, possible that we have almost reached the limit of progress in that direction—a limit set by the nature of the mechanism of the hearing apparatus itself, even if the higher brain processes are capable of further modification.

We have seen now that there may be more truth than at first appears in the paradox "everything that is new is ugly." Familiarity is an essential element of the idea of beauty. This, of course, is a wide principle and applies to much more than music.

The changes in the attitude of most persons towards new fashions in dress is another obvious example. At first they are found extreme and ugly, then tolerable, then beautiful and essential. As we saw in the experiments with pictures, some degree of familiarity is also necessary for that facilitation of attention which is so essential for æsthetic enjoyment. The repeated presentation of a good picture frequently made it more pleasing. The first time we read a difficult poem our minds may be largely occupied with discovering the meaning; when this is familiar, we can enjoy better the beauty of language and of the form of the poem. The principle is shown perhaps best of all in the appreciation of complicated musical compositions. Even an expert musician often refuses to judge a new symphony on the first hearing. It is only when he has mastered the main themes, when he is so familiar with them that he can recognise them when presented in varying guise, when he can find unity in variety, that he thoroughly enjoys the music. On the other hand, the principle obviously has its limits. Constant repetition generally produces boredom and even disgust, except perhaps in the case of the very finest works of art. And there have been cases in which music, which has stood the test of time, has been acclaimed with enthusiasm even on its first rendering, for example, the first performance in Vienna of Beethoven's Ninth Symphony.

CHAPTER IX.

MUSIC AND RHYTHM.

An Experimental Test of the Expressiveness of Music.—Can music be called the language of the emotions? Does a given musical composition express similar feelings for all, or at least for all who appreciate it intensely? In order to put this to the test, Mr. B. I. Gilman arranged an experimental concert at Boston (U.S.A.) at which a number of first-class compositions were played by well-known musicians. Mr. Gilman sent out notices to a number of people, explaining the object of the concert and inviting those who were willing to take part. About thirty responded, none professional musicians. Half of these had no skill in playing any instrument, but apparently all were capable of enjoying music keenly. Before each piece was played a certain question was put to the hearers, and they were asked to write down their answers after the piece was finished. Here are some of the questions—

Question I. Give any image that is strikingly suggested to your mind by the course of the following piece (Beethoven's Pianoforte Prelude in F Minor). Question IV. The following music has been said to tell a certain story. What dramatic suggestion do you find in it (Chopin, Ballade No. 2 in F Major, Op. 38)? Question IX. Can you connect the following melody with any marked type of personal character?

Mr. Gilman starts with the assumption that in two respects music is almost certain to be suggestive. Rhythm obviously suggests movement, and any marked type of rhythm will suggest an appropriate movement; thus triple time will suggest dancing. His second assumption is that the minor third will always be found melancholy—an assumption not borne out by his own experiments, and which my experiments with intervals showed to be incorrect.

In summarising his results Mr. Gilman concludes that there was very little agreement between the various members of the audience as to the nature of the idea or feelings expressed by the music. Thus, if we consider the first piece, the Beethoven Prelude in F Minor, which to Mr. Gilman expressed " deep gloom " or " intense energy," about half the subjects found it " dark in emotional tone " and half found it bright, though in a minor key; while as to energy, only to a small minority was great energy suggested, while several felt that *mild* energy was expressed, one referring to " the stillness of the wood." The only point of general agreement (twenty out of thirty mention it) is the suggestion of " recurrent activity without progress." Of this Mr. Gilman remarks: " If recurrent activity without progress is all the expression, import, spiritual content of the piece, it is a question whether it should be said to have any expressiveness at all, for it may be claimed that this much is in the music itself. It *is* recurrently active, and at least in the fifth bar from the end (beyond which its figure may be said simply to die away) comes round again to exactly the texture of tone that constitutes its opening bar."

It seems to me a mistake to ask in experiments of this type such definite questions as " What image is suggested ? " or " What type of character is suggested ? " They are likely to guide the attitude of the listener, and are probably partly responsible for the number of definite ideas and pictures suggested by the first piece. Mr. Gilman himself thinks it might be well to leave the hearer entirely without definite questions. He gave them because he feared he might not otherwise get enough material. When the question was very general we find some extraordinary variations, quite contradictory impressions being made by the same piece. Thus we get the following comments in answer to Question III., " What is the main impression produced by the following passage taken as a whole (Beethoven's Pianoforte Sonata in D, Op. 28—the ' Pastoral ' sonata) ? " :—

SUBJECT M. (Man).—" It puzzles me. Suggests something slightly frivolous. A comic opera."

SUBJECT H. (Woman).—" The joyful uplifting of an oppressed soul that feels itself released from depths of anguish through faith in a kind, heavenly Father."

SUBJECT J. (Man).—" Gave me a feeling of light-heartedness."

SUBJECT F. (Woman).—" A vague expression of regret."

Probably these great variations can be explained partly by the fact that one person would note especially one part of the musical composition and another person another part, and many of the pieces given would include parts of very different natures.

In some experiments of my own this last difficulty had been avoided by the playing of only short portions of compositions. I played the following selections on the piano to small groups of people :—

(a) Mendelssohn. *Songs Without Words*, 44, Bars 1–13.

(b) Portion of *Marche Romaine*—a type of piece in martial style suitable for very young players.

(c) Schubert. *Momens Musicaux*, Op. 94, No. 3, Bars 1–18.

(d) Beethoven. *Sonata* in C sharp minor (" Moonlight "), Bars 1–15.

(*e*) Beethoven. *Sonata*, Op. 26. First movement, Bars 1–17.

(*f*) Sullivan. *Mikado*. Madrigal.

No doubt with such short selections one would lose
much of the full effect of the whole compositions,
but there is less diversity within the small part. The
people who took part in these experiments, about
forty in all, were the same as those who judged the
musical chords. My object was partly to see if the
four types (character, subjective, &c.) appeared in
the appreciation of music, and partly to get some
analysis of the various kinds of experiences different
people enjoy in listening to music. (I was not
aware then of Mr. Gilman's experiments.)

It should be noted that there were no guiding
questions given such as Mr. Gilman used. The subjects were simply asked to describe their experiences
as fully and as carefully as possible. They were
students already practised to some extent in introspection.

These experiments certainly confirm Mr. Gilman's
result as to the diversity of impressions. But some
of the more careful observers give us further light
on these variations, which will, I think, be recognised
as true by all lovers of music. It is that the same
piece of music may give us one kind of impression
at one time and a quite different one on another
occasion—and not only then, but almost immediately after at the same sitting, so evanescent are the
feelings stirred by music. These diversities may be
partly due to different associations suggested by the
music. Thus one subject writes of *a:* " At the
very beginning I could scarcely resist the impulse
to get up and do something—not sit inactive, merely
listening. It suggested a lovely gavotte which I
am fond of, and yet it also suggested a feeling which
is experienced when a voluntary is started in church

and I have to come out while it is being played." It is not difficult to understand that the same piece may suggest a gavotte and a church voluntary, and once these different associations are suggested it is easy to see that they may lead to very different feelings.

Perhaps the most striking result elicited by the experiments is the large amount of visual imagery and of definite associations suggested by the music. I do not think many of my subjects were very musical as regards either accomplishment or even appreciation, though they all seemed to enjoy the music. I should certainly expect, from my own experience and from inquiries of those who are deeply moved by music, that there is as a rule little suggested in the way of visual imagery or definite association. Indeed the experiments confirm the earlier experiments with the chords in suggesting that the associative judgment (other than the formal musical association) is of low æsthetic value. There are exceptions, however, and it may be that we have a hint of keen musical feeling in the following association: " (a) reminds me of a walk I had by the sea on Sunday night when everything was still, and nothing was heard but the tune which the bells of a church were sounding out. The effect I cannot describe for it was inexpressible ! " As regards the musical and æsthetic value of this experience much depends upon whether the music recalled the tune of the bells—and *hence* the associated feeling experienced on the Sunday evening walk; or whether it stirred *directly* a similar " inexpressible " emotion, resembling that awakened by the evening bells, in which latter case probably the musical appreciation proper would be much greater and of a higher æsthetic value.

One type of imagery which we find very prominent in these experiments is imagery of movement. Repeatedly I find subjects saying they feel impelled to get up and move, especially in response to the March (*b*). Thus : " (*b*) caused a feeling of joy, and made me want to smile and jump up." " I can feel myself marching to the tune." " I felt the inclination to beat time with my foot very predominant, and could scarcely restrain the motion."

Nearly every subject experiences strong motor impulses or vivid auditory imagery in reference to (*b*), and often these are felt with other pieces. Several felt the impulse to laugh in response to the tripping cheerfulness of (*c*), two write that they laughed aloud, and one remarks, " I found it difficult to restrain myself from jumping up and making a fool of myself."

In making a final estimate of these introspective analyses I must remark that either they are very inadequate accounts of the experiences of the subjects (and of typical experiences in musical appreciation), or their experiences were not of a very high æsthetic value, whether owing to the subjects themselves or to my playing. All these causes may have contributed ; but I should imagine that most keen lovers of music would say—as Gilman himself suggests—that what music expresses is the otherwise inexpressible, or that at least to a very considerable extent it cannot be uttered in words, only in music itself. No doubt the same applies to pictorial art. Yet this does not prevent us from saying that certain descriptions of our experiences are partially fitting and accurate and others entirely wrong. And when A says that a certain piece is sad, and B says it is cheerful, each may at least be certain that the other's description would not suit his feelings. Hence we can conclude that interpretations and introspective records justify us at least in emphasising the enormous individual variations in musical experiences. On the other hand, other experiments have shown that a great composition (*e.g.* Chopin's *Funeral March*) with a very definite emotional tone may stir similar feelings in a score or more of individuals at the same time.

Music, no doubt, is a language in which a great composer can speak to others, and sometimes others understand it as he meant it. As Romain Rolland says of Beethoven : " When we are saddened by worldly miseries, it is he who comes near to us, as he used to go and play to a mother in grief, and without uttering a word thus console her by the song of his own plaintive resignation. And when we are utterly exhausted in the eternal battle use-lessly waged against mediocrity, vice, and virtue, it is an unspeakable boon to find fresh strength in this ocean-torrent of strong will and faith." These " words of consolation," however, are felt quite other-wise by some, even when they are keenly enjoyed, while to some, unhappily, they mean nothing. Still, the same is often true of verbal language ; so the dif-ference between music and words, as regards express-iveness, is after all perhaps only one of degree.

The Pleasingness of Vocal Sounds.—In order to find out whether vocal sounds, especially vowel sounds, had any definite and regular character and beauty, one experimenter asked for judgments from fifteen subjects (all women) upon various vocal sounds made by herself. It was found that the *u* sound (as in mud) was easily the least popular, eight subjects liking it less than any of the other sounds. The *a* (father) was the most pleasing, closely followed by *e* (get) and *o* (go). *Oi* (toil) was last but one, five subjects finding it less pleasing than *u* (mud). One subject, however (what nationality, I wonder ?), found *oi* the most pleasing of all. Among conso-nants *l*, *m*, and *n* were the most pleasing, while *g* and *k* were the least pleasing. It was evident that association had a good deal to do with determining the judgments. But there may be something more fundamental in some cases. For example, the *u* sound appears in the natural expression of disgust, usually written " Ugh ! "

Rhythm.—The study of rhythm is important for æsthetics owing to its prominence both in music and verse. Rhythm seems to be a very fundamental element in our mental life. In performing any regularly recurrent actions, we almost invariably tend to fall into a rhythm. It has been shown experimentally that when a series of sounds is made (for example, by an electric telephone), exactly equal in loudness and duration, the human mind is impelled to read a rhythm into the series, so that certain notes seem emphasised, and hence louder, and the intervals seem unequal. The experiment can be made in a simple form by tapping with a pencil in irregular groups of beats (thus, —′ — —′ — — — —′ — — —′ — —′ — — — — —′ —; accenting the selected beats only slightly) in the presence of a number of people. I have found that a regular rhythm is usually read into such an irregular series by every person, most saying the beats gave trochees, — u — u, others dactyls, — u u — u u, others finding an accent only every fourth beat. Most people find it much easier to imagine a two-group rhythm or a four-group rhythm than a three-group, while a five group is harder still.

This feeling for rhythm is evidently very fundamental. Little children love rhythmic sounds and noises. They often enjoy even poetry which is largely beyond their understanding if it is read with a marked rhythm.

The importance of rhythm in some forms of primitive music is well illustrated by the very interesting phonographic and other records of music obtained by Dr. C. S. Myers among the Sarawak Malays. Their orchestra consisted of (1) seven small gongs,

(2) a large gong, (3) two small drums (*a* and *b*), and (4) a still larger gong (*tawak*). Numbers 1, 2, and 3 always kept excellent time together with one another, and together they give the following scheme of beats :—

```
(1)      U U U U|U U U U|U U U U|
(2)      -       |-       |-       |
(3) (a) -    U  |-    U  |-    U  |
    (b)   U  U |  U  U |  U  U |
```

The two drums (3) are called " mother " and " child " and are beaten alternately.

The largest gong, *tawak*, was beaten in an extraordinarily complicated rhythm, which Dr. Myers, though himself an expert musician, was quite unable to unravel. " On one occasion," he writes, " the player of the *tawak* becoming tired, he passed on the instrument to another Malay, who proceeded to beat it just as a European would do, keeping strict time with the orchestra. He was laughed at by his audience, and very soon retired covered with ridicule. It was evident that only an expert could play it."

By means of a special apparatus Dr. Myers was able to obtain a record of this rhythm. He got the drummer to tap the same rhythm on a Morse key. These taps were recorded by means of connecting wires and pointer on the smoked surface of paper stretched round a revolving brass drum. These records could be made permanent by varnishing. It was only after prolonged analysis of the records that Dr. Myers was able to get the key to the rhythm, which then proved to be an exceedingly complicated one, quite incomprehensible to European ears.

Such primitive music has apparently developed along the lines of more and more complicated rhythm, while our European music has developed along the lines of more and more complicated harmonies, though rhythm too has of course developed with us. It would seem possible that rhythm may develop still more in our European music. Early training in rhythmic movements—such, for example, as that given by the Eurythmics of M. Dalcroze—enables children to move their arms in a certain rhythm and to dance at the same time in a different rhythm, a feat which the untrained adult usually finds quite impossible.

As we have seen, habituation to novel harmonies enables surprising novelties to be enjoyed after a time. When the simple and more fundamental rhythms are mastered, so that they can be followed in a subconscious way, attention can be focussed on more complicated rhythmic forms accompanying these fundamental rhythms. To the expert these in turn become easy of apprehension. For full æsthetic enjoyment this is necessary ; for music, like other forms of art we have discussed, must conform to the principle of facilitation of attention.

In the tones which in themselves can so deeply appeal to us, music already possesses a powerful mode of stimulation. When these form a recurring series of impulses the effects can be heightened. For not only does rhythm make its fundamental appeal to our feelings, with its suggestions of free and joyous movement, but the arrangement of the tone impressions in regular rhythmic form enables us to apprehend them in groups, and so respond to a far greater stimulus than would otherwise be possible, without confusion of mind.

On page 97, in summing up our previous findings, we concluded that in the æsthetic experience there must be adequate change to maintain interest and to stimulate intellectual activity. In music, when the rhythm is simple, the variety is supplied by the movements in the melody and the changing harmonies. In the Malay music, with an absence of melody and harmony, change was supplied by much more varied rhythms. And "as in the apprehension of a beautiful curve one part gives us a clue to the nature of the rest," so the apprehension of the rhythmic form of a piece of music enables us to receive the rest of the music in a mental attitude of repose which would be impossible if the notes followed in irregular order, or if a new rhythm appeared every few bars. Music thus, in a very marked degree, satisfies the formula which one writer has offered as the definition of æsthetic experience—namely, the combining at the same time of "stimulation with repose." *

* E. D. Puffer in the *Psychology of Beauty*.

REFERENCES FOR FURTHER READING.

THERE is no other book in English known to the present writer devoted to this branch of Experimental Psychology. Excellent chapters on the subject will be found in the " Introduction to Experimental Psychology," by C. S. Myers (Cambridge Manuals of Science and Literature, 1911, 1s. net), and in " Experimental Psychology and Culture," by G. M. Stratton (Macmillan, 1903, 10s. 6d. net). Either of these books will also provide an admirable introduction to other branches of Experimental Psychology. I should like to say here that Chap. IV. of this little book owes much to Professor Stratton's lucid chapter upon the " Enjoyment of Sensations."

On the general psychology of Æsthetics " The Psychology of Beauty," by E. D. Puffer (Constable, 1907) can be recommended.

For the sake of the student and of those who wish to read further in any special department, a list of books and articles is appended.

CHAPTER I.—GENERAL SURVEY OF METHODS AND RESULTS.

O. Külpe. " Der gegenwärtige Stand der experimentellen Ästhetik," in the *Bericht d. II Kongr. für Exp. Psych.* Leipzig, 1907. An excellent review up to date.

C. Lalo. " L'Esthétique Experimentale Contemporaine." Paris, 1908. Felix Alcan, 3 frs. 50 cs. Does not deal much with recent experimental work.

CHAPTERS II. AND III.

Ch. Féré. " Sensation et Movement." Paris, Felix Alcan, 1900.

C. S. Myers. " Some Observations on the Development of the Colour Sense," *British Journal of Psychology*, 1908, vol. ii. 353.

W. McDougall. " An Investigation of the Colour Sense of Two Infants," *Ibid.*, 338.

C. W. Valentine. " The Colour Perception and Colour Preferences of an Infant during its Fourth and Eighth Month," *Brit. Journ. of Psych.*, vol. vi.

M. W. Shinn. " The Development of the Senses in the First Three Years of Childhood," *Univ. of California Publications*, 1907.

W. H. Winch. "Colour Preferences of School-Children," *Brit. Journ. of Psych.*, vol. iii.

E. Bullough. "The Apparent Heaviness of Colours," *Brit. Journ. of Psych.*, vol. ii.

E. Bullough. "The Perceptive Problem in the Æsthetic Appreciation of Single Colours," *Brit. Journ. of Psych.*, vol. ii.

E. Bullough. "The Perceptive Problem in the Æsthetic Appreciation of Simple Colour-Combinations." *Brit. Journ. of Psych.*, vol. iii.

Clark, Goodall, and Washburn. "The Effect of Area on the Pleasantness of Colours," *American Journal of Psychology.* Oct. 1911.

Crawford and Washburn. "Fluctuations in the Affective Value of Colours during Fixation for one Minute," *Ibid.*

Major. "On the Affective Tone of Simple Sense Impressions," *Amer. Journ. of Psych.*, vol. vii.

I. Powerson and M. Washburn. "The Effect of Suggestion on the Affective Value of Colour," *Amer. Journ. of Psych.* April 1912.

CHAPTERS IV. AND V.

L. Martin. "An Experimental Study of Fechner's Principles," *Psychological Review*, vol. xiii., 1906.

G. M. Stratton. "Experimental Psychology and Culture," Chap. 12.

T. Lipps. "Æsthetische Factoren der Raumanschauung," in *Beiträge*, published as Festgruss to Helmholtz, 1891.

C. W. Valentine. "Psychological Theories of the Horizontal-Vertical Illusion," *Brit. Journ. of Psych.*, vol. ii.

T. H. Haines and A. E. Davies. "The Psychology of Æsthetic Reaction to Rectangular Forms," *Psych. Review*, vol. xi.

R. P. Angier. "The Æsthetics of Unequal Division," *Psych. Review, Monograph Supplements*, vol. iv.

E. D. Puffer. "Studies in Symmetry," *Ibid.*

Jacob Segal. "Beiträge zur exper. Ästhetik," *Archiv für die Gesamte Psych.*, VII Band.

L. W. Legowski. "Beiträge zur exper. Ästhetik," *Archiv f. d. Gesamte Psych.*, XII Band.

CHAPTERS VI. AND VII.

R. Schulze. "Die Mimik der Kinder beim künstlerischen Geniessen." Leipzig, 1906.

E. Meumann. "Experimentelle Pädagogik" (2nd edition), *Achte Vorlesung.*

M. W. Calkins. "An Attempted Experiment in Psychological Æsthetics," *Psych. Review*, vol. vii., 1900.

L. J. Martin. " An Experimental Study of Fechner's Principles "
    (as above).
L. J. Martin. " Experimental Prospecting in the Fields of
    the Comic," *Amer. Journ. of Psych.*, vol. xvi., 1905.
O. Külpe. " Ein Beitrag zur experimentellen Æsthetik," *Amer.
    Journ. of Psych.*, vol. xiv., 1903.
E. von Ritook. " Zur Analyse der ästhetischen Wirkung auf
    Grund der Methode der Zeitvariation." *Zeitschrift für
    Æsthetik und allgemeine Kunstwissenschaft* (Max Dessoir),
    V Band.

CHAPTERS VIII. AND IX.

R. McDougall. " The Structure of Simple Rhythm Forms,"
    Psych. Review, Monograph Supplements, vol. iv.
R. H. Stetson. " Rhythm and Rhyme," *Ibid.*
C. S. Myers. " Study of Rhythm in Primitive Music," *Brit.
    Journ. of Psych.*, vol. i.
M. Meyer. " Musical Æsthetics," *Amer. Journ. of Psych.*,
    vol. xiv.
B. I. Gilman. " An Experimental Test of Musical Expressive-
    ness." *Amer. Journ. of Psych.*, vols. iv. and v.
C. W. Valentine. " The Æsthetic Appreciation of Musical
    Intervals among School-Children and Adults," *Brit. Journ.
    of Psych.*, vol. vi.
C. S. Myers (with contributions by C. W. Valentine). " A
    Study of Individual Differences in the Attitude towards
    Tones." *Brit. Journ. of Psych.*, vol. vii., 1914.
C. W. Valentine. " The Method of Comparison in Experiments
    with Musical Intervals and the Effect of Practice on the
    Appreciation of Discords." *Brit. Journ. of Psych.*, vol.
    vii., 1914.

INDEX.

PRINTED IN GREAT BRITAIN AT
THE PRESS OF THE PUBLISHERS.